QUEENS OF CRIME

QUEENS OF CRIME

TRUE STORIES OF WOMEN CRIMINALS FROM INDIA

SUSHANT SINGH
KULPREET YADAV

EBURY
PRESS

An imprint of Penguin Random House

EBURY PRESS

USA | Canada | UK | Ireland | Australia
New Zealand | India | South Africa | China | Singapore

Ebury Press is part of the Penguin Random House group of companies
whose addresses can be found at global.penguinrandomhouse.com

Published by Penguin Random House India Pvt. Ltd
4th Floor, Capital Tower 1, MG Road,
Gurugram 122 002, Haryana, India

First published in Ebury Press by Penguin Random House India 2019

10 9 8 7 6 5 4 3 2

ISBN 9780143445852

Typeset in Dante MT Std by Manipal Digital Systems, Manipal

Printed at Manipal Technologies Limited, India

www.penguin.co.in

Contents

Contents

1

The Drug Queen Of Mumbai

The abusive husband pushed his wife out of the house. 'Get out, bitch! I don't want to see your dirty face ever again.' He threw a bundle of clothes after her and slammed the door shut.

The woman, who was in her early twenties, picked up the bundle and started to walk away from the house, located in one of the many slums of Mumbai. She didn't look back.

With her two young sons gripping an index finger each, the end of a loveless marriage was not what was troubling her—it was the end of the relationship. *What will I do all by myself?* She was worried about food and shelter for the three of them.

The woman's name was Shantidevi Patkar. On that rainy day in 1982, as she walked in the drizzle, past vada-pav stalls and women selling jasmine garlands on the roadside, she was nobody but a faceless Mumbaikar who was poor, unwanted and worthless.

Shantidevi decided to go to Siddharth Nagar chawl in Mumbai's Worli area. It was the first place that came to her mind as she had grown up there. As soon as she reached the chawl with her children, the familiar sights, sounds and smells greeted her and brought back traces of a smile to her face. She had lived there as a little girl before marriage pulled her away from her world, which comprised her parents and five brothers. Since she was the only sister in a family of boys, she had been pampered a lot.

Back in Siddharth Nagar, her sons on either side, she wondered which door to knock on first. Four of her five brothers were married and living in their own rooms. She decided to stay in the room of her brother who was serving time in jail for murder. Two of her other brothers had served jail sentences for the same murder, but they were out now. Another brother, who had been arrested initially but had had nothing to do with the crime, had committed suicide in jail in protest.

She knocked on the door, the awkwardness of the moment weighing her down. The door, which led to a small eight-by-eight-foot room, was opened by her brother's wife, Sumiti.

'Didi! What a pleasant surprise! Welcome,' her sister-in-law greeted her and pulled the children into an embrace. She had been married for just a few months and didn't have any children of her own.

Sumiti was quick to realize that something was amiss. After serving them tea, she said, 'Didi, I'm with you. You don't have to say anything.'

Her affection brought tears to Shantidevi's eyes. 'Thank you.'

The next morning, her sister-in-law left the house early, before Shantidevi woke up. But she had prepared a kadai full of poha for the three of them. Shantidevi woke her children up, helped them bathe outside using the bucket of water that had been kept ready for them, and then all of them ate gratefully.

That evening, Shantidevi asked her sister-in-law, 'Can I get work here?'

Sumiti nodded. 'I've already spoken to a lady in one of the apartment complexes not far from here. She will give you two hundred rupees for two hours. I'll get you more houses to work in within a week.'

Shantidevi thanked her again. She was grateful because now she could earn her own money. It was the economic empowerment that she needed.

Soon, Shantidevi was working in three houses and was able to move into her own room in the same chawl. Now that she was earning Rs 600, she could hire a room for Rs 300.

Her life was unremarkable for the next year. She was barely able to make ends meet with the meagre salary that she earned. Her husband never bothered to check if she was all right. He was so heartless, thought Shantidevi, that he didn't even inquire about the children. The lack of money started to pinch her. But what could an uneducated woman like her do?

One day, something unexpected happened. As she was walking back home along the Worli Sea Face after work, she felt weak and decided to stop for a few minutes at a bus stop nearby to catch her breath. She sat on the metal bench, held the pillar for support and closed her eyes. It is just weakness, she thought, and will pass soon. It did, and after a minute or so when she opened her eyes, she found that a man seated at the far end of the bench was staring at her.

She was about to give him a mouthful to nip whatever he had in his mind in the bud, but the man spoke first, 'Sister, the world can be cruel. Are you feeling better now?'

His voice calmed her down, as did the fact that he had addressed her as 'sister'. She nodded and wondered if she should get up and be on her way.

But before she could, the man spoke again, 'And in Mumbai, there is only one god. Do you know who that is?'

'Ganpati bappa.'

He laughed and then, his face turning serious, said, 'No, the real god is money, cash, rupiya.'

The man was crazy, thought Shantidevi.

'If you have the money, everything is great. But if you don't have the money, you live the life of an insect in this city.'

A grasshopper flew out of nowhere and landed near his feet. The man raised his Kolhapuri chappal and stamped on it. 'This guy here had no money, so I ended his life.'

She smiled for the first time. The man was right. She said, 'But for money you need an education. Insects are uneducated.'

'Says who? What if I told you that the man who lives on the tenth floor of this building,' he paused and pointed towards a posh building behind them before continuing, 'in flat number 1002, is uneducated and yet he is rich.'

'That's a lie.'

'That's not a lie, sister. I work for that man, which is why I know.'

Shantidevi got up and walked towards him. She sat on a bench three feet from him, saying, 'How is that even possible, brother? Tell me about him.'

Little did Shantidevi know that this conversation would change her life. The man identified himself as a drug peddler and said that his boss was once a drug peddler too. But that was ten years ago. Now he was the boss and controlled a drug business that generated several crores.

'But this is a crime. Why should I get involved in this dirty work?'

'You wash utensils. Is that not dirty work? You clean floors. Is that not dirty work? You wash clothes. Is that not dirty work? And how much money do you make in a month doing these dirty things? One thousand?'

'Are you out of your mind? I make only six hundred.'

'In the dirty work that I'm talking about, you can make ten thousand in one month.'

'But what about the police? Don't you fear them?'

The man laughed. 'We pay the police to look the other way.'

'Impossible.'

'Sister, you are so naïve. Don't you want to make more money? What you make in one year can be made in just one month.'

She kept quiet for a while, not knowing how to respond. The man got up and said, 'I respect you. I must go now. Remember, we never had this conversation.'

'No, wait. I see your point and I want the money, but I have two small children. If I'm caught, their future will be ruined.'

'What future? Do you think they will have a future if they go to a municipality school?'

Shantidevi was quiet again. She knew that what the man was suggesting was something bad, something that didn't have the sanction of God, something that was immoral. She stared out at the sea. But she soon realized that whatever name people might give to that kind of work, it would bring money.

'I'm a woman, brother, and a woman should know her limits. A woman should never step beyond her limits. My husband used to say this.'

'Where is your husband now?'

'He threw me out of the house.'

'And you still pay heed to what he said to you? Sister, you truly are strange.'

It was Shantidevi's turn now to get to her feet. The man had said something that needed deeper thought. He had, perhaps without knowing it, offered her a perspective that was the opposite of the principles her husband used to preach. It was now between what her husband thought was right and what she thought was right.

'I'll see you tomorrow at the same time here. By then I will have decided.'

She walked away, her head held a notch higher, murmuring, 'Ten thousand in one month?'

That night, Shantidevi couldn't sleep. The numbers kept echoing in her mind along with every other word that the man had said. The next evening, he was at the bus stop.

She walked towards him, looked him in the eye and said, 'Yes, I want to do this. Tell me what I have to do.'

'Thank you, sister. I promise you will not regret it.'

Shantidevi started at the lowest rung. Her task was to peddle brown sugar and hashish. A daily target was set and her beat covered five-star hotels across the city. She learnt the ropes fast. There was a huge demand and she was quick to realize that the supply was barely enough to keep pace with it. Her customers trusted her more because she was a woman. She never cheated anyone, keeping the pricing as explained. Within two years, she had made enough money to buy her own small room in the chawl. Her sons were now studying in an English-medium school and her life began to change for the better.

The year was 1985 and Rajiv Gandhi's Congress party had just won the general elections with their best margin ever. Over the Atlantic Ocean, half a world away, terrorists had detonated a bomb on Air India flight 181, killing all 329 people on board. But these events had no bearing on Shantidevi. She had found a new way to make money and she was focusing all her energy on it.

The man who had introduced her to the drug trade disappeared after a couple of years. But by then Shantidevi had learnt enough about the business, and soon, she was operating on her own. She would collect the consignment herself, transporting it in a taxi to her chawl. As the taxi could not negotiate the narrow lanes inside, she hired men to collect the gunny bags and deliver them to her room, which sat on top of a hillock within the chawl.

To act as mules, she hired twenty young men; almost all of them drug addicts. The addicts got their fix for free and usually died on the job within one to two years of recruitment. But by then they had spread the poison to many others, and Shantidevi would pick the best among them to act as new mules.

One afternoon, sometime in 1992, Shantidevi, who was alone in her room, opened the door to a knock and found a constable standing there. It was her first direct confrontation with the police, and her initial reaction was one of horror. There were many kilograms of drugs in her room at that time and a lot of money too. In fact, she was making so much money that she had stopped counting it almost a year ago.

'I want to search your house,' demanded the policeman, steel in his voice.

Shantidevi mustered her courage, cocked her hip suggestively, placed a hand on the door frame and said, 'Only the house? You are welcome to search me too.'

The policeman's expression changed. She extended her hand and touched his face, tracing a line across his face and lips with her finger. Then she winked at him.

He stepped forward and entered the small room. It was noon and no one was expected for the next hour.

He stepped closer and, grabbing her waist, pulled her towards him.

'I'm all yours,' she murmured.

The man began to kiss her, and as she responded, he was filled with a fire she had never known a man to possess for a woman. Soon they were having sex. When it was over, she asked him, 'Are you satisfied with your search?'

He smiled. 'Someone informed us that there are a lot of drugs here.'

'I'm that drug, sahib. You will get addicted to me in no time.'

He looked around, seemed satisfied and, after promising to come back soon, left the house. As soon as he was gone, Shantidevi breathed easy. But she knew that she would have to do something about the drugs in her house immediately. That very day, she bought another room close to her own using some of the cash that she had accumulated. The room could not be accessed from anywhere except from the roof of another room. She had the entire consignment of drugs shifted there.

The constable, whose name was Ajay Lokhande, started to visit her every week. Soon the two of them became close. Sometimes she went with him to different parts of the city for ice cream. It was as if not just him, but the woman in her was also addicted to the man.

One day, he said, 'Shantidevi, you can't fool me. I knew all about you from the first day. But I have not said anything because I have fallen in love with you.'

They were sitting on Juhu beach, eating pav bhaji. His declaration initially made her uncomfortable, but then she said, 'Why don't you help me make more money? You can have some for yourself too. What does the police job pay you, after all?'

From that moment on, Lokhande became her partner. She even started to use his official police jeep to send drug consignments across the city as it was not stopped and checked en route.

Even after paying a handsome commission to Lokhande, her coffers continued to fill. Soon, there was so much money that it was impossible to keep it without attracting the attention of other criminals. One of her brothers, who had been released from jail and was now helping her, said one evening, his voice serious, 'We need to do something about the money.'

The same thought had been on Shantidevi's mind. 'I know, but we can't put it in a bank as they will ask us where we got the money from.'

'Let's start a business, say, a taxi service. That way, we can deposit a few thousand rupees every day, saying we have earned it.'

She smiled at her brother, took a bite of the vada pav he had bought for her, sipped her tea and said with a full mouth, 'Smart brother.'

'But one bank account will not be enough. Let me see how many accounts all of us can open without raising suspicion.'

She swallowed, took another bite, another sip of tea and repeated, 'Smart brother.'

Within the next few weeks, Shantidevi had a legitimate taxi business. Her extended family had successfully opened twenty-nine bank accounts. Finally, she had better control over her finances. But soon, even the accounts could not hold the kind of money she was making. So she started to buy gold ornaments. And after she had had enough of gold, she turned to real estate.

In March 2001, her luck finally ran out and she was caught with 30 grams of hashish. The arrest cost her dearly. She had to spend almost eight months in jail before she was released on bail.

On her return, she stomped into her room and called her team for a meeting. She had checked the accounts and found that profits had dropped by 80 per cent. Shantidevi shouted at everyone, 'Bastards, you can't even do this much without me. You have ruined my business.'

'Didi,' one of her brothers tried to protest, but as soon as her eyes fell on him, he fell quiet.

It took her just a few weeks to gather the information she needed. Many new people had encroached on her distribution areas and it was time for her to teach them a lesson. She sent a message to Lokhande. When he arrived, they left for a two-day trip to Khandala.

As soon as they had settled into their hotel room, she said, her voice serious, 'I want these bastards out of our areas.'

Lokhande took a deep breath and said, 'There is only one way. You should become a police informer.'

'Police informer? Is there such a thing?'

'Yes. I will convince my headquarters to use you; I will tell them that you are a credible source, that you have a lot of connections and would like to make money by selling information. That will not be difficult for me. Apart from this, my current appointment with the intelligence wing of the Mumbai Police will ensure that the information you provide is acted upon.'

Her eyes sparkled. She waited for him to continue.

'Tell your boys to find out what your competitors are up to and then give that information to the police. They will not only be arrested, but their drugs will also be torched.'

'But what if my rivals find out who is doing this? Won't they come after me?'

'No. The police protect the identity of their informers. Otherwise, who would risk their ass, madam?'

Shantidevi laughed. Lokhande knew that he had scored a brownie point and pulled her towards him to redeem it immediately.

During the next few years, Shantidevi not only won her territory back, but also had most of her competitors arrested. This allowed her to expand her area of operations. Soon she was controlling all of Mumbai city and had a team of more than 100 mules. By then, both her sons had also joined her business and, along with her brothers, they executed the crucial role of supervision and control.

As her profits multiplied, her clout also began to grow. She invested in a few local politicians, and some of them even won elections. One such person was a middle-aged factory-worker-turned-union-leader called Ramsaheb Bhau. Since his campaign for the Brihanmumbai Mahanagar Palika election had been funded by her, the first person he visited to seek blessings after he won was Shantidevi.

'Didi, thank you,' he beamed as soon as she opened the door. By now, she had conjoined four rooms in the chawl, creating a house. The guests were attended to in the first room, in which four blue velvet armchairs were arranged in a semicircle around a three-seater sofa of the same colour. A glass table was placed in front of the sofa and a television sat in one corner of the room. The walls were bare and a strong smell of disinfectant hung in the air.

Shantidevi sat in the centre of the sofa and signalled Ramsaheb to take a seat. He approached slowly, bowing out of respect, and settled on the edge of the sofa.

'Didi, thank you.'

'You don't have to thank me. It's all your work.'

He signalled to the man who had come with him and stood right behind him holding a box of sweets. The man handed the box over to Ramsaheb and the young politician opened the box and took out a sweet. He paused as he looked at Shantidevi, his hand half extended, and smiled. 'Madam, for you. Please bless me.'

'Why are you calling me madam? I'm just your sister.' There was mild admonishment in her voice.

The politician looked worried at the gaffe but when Shantidevi smiled, he leant forward and as she opened her mouth, placed the sweet in it. There was silence as she chewed and when she had finally swallowed, he got to his feet, 'Didi, I will take your leave now. Please let me know if I can be of help at any stage.'

She nodded and he bowed and left with his assistant. The experience gave Shantidevi a new high. She had finally found a safer place to invest her overflowing money. There would be many more in need of money for elections, she reckoned.

A few months later, the unthinkable happened. A woman, Asha Kashikar, who lived with her two sons in a room not far from hers, started selling drugs as well. Shantidevi was aghast. This was competition right under her nose. Since she knew the woman well, she decided to talk some sense into her.

She walked across to Kashikar's house one morning. The lady invited her inside and said, 'Didi, would you like to have tea?'

Shantidevi came straight to the point, 'I know what you are doing. I want you to stop.'

The woman, in a display of nerve that Shantidevi thought she didn't have, tucked the *pallu* of her sari into her petticoat and asked, 'Who are you to ask me to stop?'

Shantidevi had always liked the woman so she kept her calm. 'See, if you have to do this, you will have to operate in another area. I have paid too high a price to build my business. I don't want it to be ruined.'

'Why don't you leave, you whore!'

The conversation was clearly not going Shantidevi's way. Beginning to get angry but still maintaining her composure, she said, 'Sister, look, I don't want any trouble. You have two options. Either you stop selling from today, or you sell somewhere else.'

'Are you threatening me, you bitch?'

'I am only advising you. I don't want any of us getting hurt.'

'Get out, you whore! I want you to leave right now.'

Shantidevi got up and walked back to her house even as she heard the woman saying, 'Let's see who wins this, you bitch.'

She considered her options. She couldn't inform the cops because that would bring them too close to her own den. The sniffer dogs would smell out her stash in no time and, along with Kashikar, her future would be ruined as well. It was now a game of survival. That night, she ordered her brother to lock Kashikar's room from the outside and set it on fire. The woman was burnt alive in her own home along with the drugs she was hoarding there.

The woman's two sons, who were not in Mumbai that night, lodged a police complaint against Shantidevi once they were back. Lokhande told her not to worry. He ensured that the complaint was not acted upon and Shantidevi's reign as the supreme leader of the Mumbai drug underworld continued.

Sometime in 2012, one of her mules received information that captured her attention. He said, 'Madam, something new has come in the market. It's called "meow meow". It has the same effect as cocaine, but it is twenty times cheaper. My customers are now asking me for meow meow.'

Shantidevi liked the name, meow meow, and soon found out more about it. Everything she learnt was music to her ears. The best thing was that the drug was not banned in India. A drug that was not illegal to procure, distribute, sell and consume. It couldn't get better than that.

She took Lokhande into confidence and the two of them started to scout for suppliers. Their search took them to Gujarat, Rajasthan and Madhya Pradesh. They entered into contracts with the factories engaged in the manufacturing of meow meow. She paid them in advance and booked their stock for the next few years. This did two things for her. First, she was able to throttle the Mumbai-based distributors of meow meow as they no longer had a source, and second, she gained total control over the business.

The mules went to work within a month of her learning about the existence of meow meow.

By the end of one year, around 70 per cent of addicts in Mumbai were hooked to meow meow. Since the drug was not a banned substance, Shantidevi's dependence on the police reduced.

A few months after Shantidevi started selling meow meow, she found out from a trusted source that Lokhande was seeing another woman. This explained his increasing lack of interest in Shantidevi. The situation was indeed a challenge because Lokhande knew a lot about her and her business. She realized that she would have to handle the problem carefully as there was simply too much at risk.

After deep thought, she took a harsh decision. It was time to grab the bull by the horns. If there was one thing that had kept Shantidevi ahead of the others during all her years in the business, it was her ability to take important decisions quickly. She had never believed in the wait-and-watch policy.

The next morning, she called the police and once again played the role of an informer. 'I have information.'

'Where have you been? We have not heard from you in years.'

'I was busy, but now I have information. Are you interested?'

'Yes, go on.'

'There is an inspector posted in the Marine Lines police station who goes by the name of Ajay Lokhande. There are a lot of drugs hidden in his house in Satara district.' She gave them the address.

The man on the other side thanked her and disconnected the phone. The game had begun. Shantidevi knew that if she played it right, she would straighten out her ex-lover.

Two days later, she read in the newspaper that Lokhande had been arrested after a big consignment of drugs was found in his home in Satara. The news report also said that the police had found a few kilograms of drugs in his locker at the Marine Lines police station. The confiscated items had been sent for testing.

She put the newspaper down, picked up her purse, hailed a taxi and ordered the driver to take her to Arthur Road Jail in Colaba, where, according to the news report, Lokhande was being held, pending his bail hearing. She reached the jail at five in the evening, the time when prisoners are allowed to meet visitors. A policeman escorted her inside. She met Lokhande in the visiting area, where he was seated behind a wire mesh that acted as a separator.

She wondered if she felt bad about the situation. The man she had loved and who had helped her for so many years was in jail because of her. She was sure he knew that she was responsible for his arrest. But she didn't feel any guilt. In fact, she didn't feel anything at all.

'Hello,' she faked a smile.

He remained silent and stared at his feet.

'I hope you have learnt your lesson?'

He nodded, looked up and tried to smile, but failed. She could hear him breathing through flared nostrils. He was angry, but so was she.

She took a deep breath and said, 'I can save you. You may not love me any more, but I am loyal.'

He didn't say anything, but he had found the nerve to stare right into her eyes. He didn't blink. Shantidevi knew he was in no position to harm her. No one would pay attention to anything he said. He was tainted for life.

She left the jail and returned to the chawl. Although Shantidevi had properties, both commercial and residential, in Mumbai, Pune and Khandala, she preferred to stay in her chawl. It was her home and no amount of money would make her leave her simple abode.

A week after her visit to Lokhande, she received a rude shock. The police named her as a co-accused in the case based on a statement made by one of Lokhande's neighbours in Satara. When shown pictures of various suspects, the neighbour, upon seeing Shantidevi's photograph, identified her as someone who used to frequent Lokhande's house.

Shantidevi was arrested once again.

But she had nothing to worry about as the drug confiscated from Satara was meow meow. She called her lawyer and told him, 'I need bail immediately. Meow meow is not banned.'

Her lawyer said, 'I agree, but I have heard that the government is trying to ban it even as we speak.'

'But surely we can have the bail hearing before that, can't we?'

'I'll try my best.'

Unfortunately for her, meow meow was banned before the hearing.

However, she was still on firm ground according to her lawyer. He pleaded to the judge on her behalf, 'My lord, I agree that meow meow has been added to the list of banned substances, but when it was confiscated in Satara, it was not classified as a drug; it was simply a chemical.'

The judge removed his spectacles and looked up from the file he was reading. 'Right, but the police have already removed Lokhande from service because of this substance. We can't give different treatment to the co-accused, can we?'

Shantidevi said to the judge, 'Sahib, the truth is that the powder that was confiscated is not meow meow.'

Her lawyer looked at her and she smiled confidently. The judge ordered proper laboratory tests to be conducted to determine what the substance that had been confiscated in Satara was. Just a police report would not do; a chemical analysis report from a government-run lab would have to be provided.

Pending the report, the judge granted Shantidevi bail with strict conditions.

After three days, Shantidevi got a call from a peon who worked in the superintendent of police's (SP) office in Satara. At the time she was at home, supervising the distribution of meow meow for the following week.

'Madam, SP sahib wants to talk to you.'

'Okay,' Shantidevi's sharp mind started working out the possibilities as she held the receiver tightly against her ear. She soon knew what was in store for her.

'Shantidevi?'

Signalling her team to carry on, she moved out of earshot and said, 'SP sahib, yes, it's me.'

'If you want to get out of this, I need five lakhs.'

She smiled as she pleaded. 'Can't you reduce it a little, sahib?'

'No. Five lakhs and I will take care of things.'

'Fine, I will give you five lakhs, sahib. Just save me this time.'

The SP then explained to her how the money was to be handed over to him, before hanging up.

Shantidevi didn't like this particular SP. She had, on an earlier occasion, given him Rs 10 lakh, but this time she was in no mood to comply with his demands.

She called the police and told them that the SP had asked her for a bribe.

The police laid a trap for the unsuspecting SP, and two days later, as she was handing over the money to him in a crowded Mumbai market, he was caught red-handed.

A week later, when the hearing for the case started, it was the turn of everyone present in the courtroom to be surprised. As per the laboratory's report, the confiscated drug turned out to be Ajinomoto, or monosodium glutamate, which is used as a flavouring agent in many Chinese dishes. The samples had been analysed by two laboratories, each in a different city, and the results were the same.

Even though it made no sense for a policeman to store such a large quantity of a food-flavouring agent in his house, no one could say anything as the hard facts were before them and when it came to the law, only facts mattered, nothing else.

Both Lokhande and Shantidevi were acquitted. They walked out of the courtroom side by side, their lawyers following them.

'I hope I never see you again,' Lokhande said through clenched teeth when they were about to part ways and head to their respective vehicles.

'Don't be so sure, super-cop.'

How the meow meow was converted into Ajinomoto overnight will always remain a mystery. If there is one person who knows what happened, it is Shantidevi, or perhaps the ex-SP of Satara.

Shantidevi, meanwhile, is still alive and well in Mumbai. Rumour has it that her empire continues to flourish.

Interesting fact: Today, if you ask anyone about Shantidevi in Worli, they will tell you that she sells the best pomfret. One interesting story that has been doing the rounds among the staff of the Narcotics Control Bureau (NCB) and Mumbai Police officers is that when Shantidevi first started in the business, she had two oversized shirts for both her sons, which had drugs stitched into them. Whenever she heard that a policeman was asking for her, she would order the boys to wear the shirts and run off. It always worked.

2

The Queen of the Dark

'Dad, you are not well. How will you drive your autorickshaw today?' sixteen-year-old Meeta asked her father, Sri Prakash. They were in their two-room house on the second floor of a building in a small colony in east Delhi's Laxmi Nagar.

'Don't worry . . . don't . . . don't worry, beta, I will do it. This is nothing.' The father looked into the eyes of his daughter who stood before him in her school uniform. He tried to smile, but another bout of coughing kept him from doing so.

Meeta's mother emerged from the small kitchen and gave her a lunch box. 'Go fast or you will miss your school bus.'

When she turned to look at her mother, Meeta had tears in her eyes.

Her mother smiled. 'Your father is fine. He will take medicines and go to work. Don't worry. I'm here to take care of him.'

'You can't take care of him, mama. We need to go to the doctor.'

'No, this is just a cough and he will be fine soon.'

Her father looked up. The bout of coughing had subsided and this time he could smile as he said, 'Meeta, this is nothing. Go to school. School is very important, beta.'

'Dad, for me, you are more important. Please don't say it's nothing. You have been coughing the whole night. We need to go to a doctor.'

Her father extended his hand and placed it on her head. Then he said affectionately, 'I work hard so that you can go to school, beta. I want you to do well in your studies and become a big government sahib.'

Meeta was not convinced and began to cry. 'Dad, I am not a child. I'm sixteen. I know we don't have money for your medicines. I will not go to school from today. We will use the school fees to take care of your hospital bills. I can rejoin next year.'

Her father's expression changed. He removed his hand from her head and spoke firmly, 'Meeta, I'm your father. I know what is best for our family. Just go to school. No arguments now.'

She turned to look at her mother, whose face had hardened too. Meeta picked up her bag and walked out of the house.

Meeta's father died two months later. Meeta and her mother were shattered. Within days, they realized that he had taken a loan of Rs 1 lakh, which had to be repaid. Not only had the family lost the sole earning member, but they had also inherited a debt that they had no means of repaying. Meeta had a younger brother and sister too. But they were too young to contribute in any way.

Two weeks after her father passed away, Meeta, who had stopped going to school, said to her mother, 'Mama, I have found a job.'

She paused and allowed the information to sink in. Meeta expected her mother to protest violently, but all she did was raise her head and look at her daughter with empty eyes. Before Meeta could elaborate, her mother had tears rolling down her cheeks.

That same evening Meeta joined a beauty parlour. It was near her house, on the third floor of an office building. Meeta's shift was from one in the afternoon to nine at night. Besides her, there were ten other girls working there. All of them were older than her. At first, she found the set-up intimidating. There were far too many lights, strange equipment that she had never seen before and lots of mirrors. The parlour also had a rather flashy name: Curvy and Dazzling Beauty.

On her first day, the owner, Rupi, introduced her to the other girls and said, 'Learn fast. After a few weeks, if I like you, I will start giving you a commission in addition to your salary. Here, meet Pinky, who will train you. Pinky has been with us for two years. She is the best.'

Rupi smiled at Pinky, who said, 'Hello, Meeta.'

'Hello,' Meeta replied and nodded at her as the owner went back to the magazine she was reading.

Pinky turned out to be the lifeline that Meeta needed. She was friendly, affectionate and patient, and had a great sense of humour. Over the next few weeks, Pinky trained Meeta.

Meeta was awed by Pinky. It was not just because of her proficiency at her job, but also the fact that Pinky appeared to be well-off. She came to work in a big car, wore expensive clothes and looked more like a model than an employee at a beauty parlour.

Meeta attributed Pinky's appearance and wealth to family money and never asked her any personal questions. She kept her head down and, after a month, when she was paid Rs 5000 as her first salary, she was ecstatic. She bought a box of sweets on her way home. She knocked on the door of her house, wearing a big smile.

The door was opened by a man she had never seen before. She walked in, confused, and looked at her mother who sat crying in a corner. There was another man seated in the room. He said, 'How much have you got?'

It took her a few seconds to understand what the man meant.

'Four thousand eight hundred.'

He got up and came close to her, 'Give it to me.'

She looked at her mother who didn't meet her eyes. Meeta knew she could not disobey these men. She opened her purse and gave them all the money she had earned.

After pocketing it, the man said, 'This is just the interest. Your one lakh stays as it is.'

This was too much for the girl who had been putting up a brave fight so far. She began to cry.

The man who had pocketed the money leant close to her and whispered, 'There are other ways to pay too.'

Although he had whispered, he had deliberately been loud enough for Meeta's mother to hear. She looked up sharply and shouted, 'Get out!'

The men looked at her, their smiles broadened, and then they looked at each other before leaving.

Meeta ran to hug her mother as soon as the door closed. The men had even taken the sweets she had bought. She had nothing. The family had nothing.

The next day at the parlour she was quiet. She had not had dinner and had skipped breakfast too despite her mother's insistence.

She was trying to focus on her work.

That afternoon, Pinky tapped her on the shoulder. When Meeta turned to look at her, she signalled her to step outside. There were no customers in the parlour and, like most afternoons, it was a slow period. Meeta followed Pinky outside. There was a coffee shop on the ground floor where they went and sat.

'Coffee?' Pinky asked her.

'No.'

'Tea?'

She shook her head.

Pinky took Meeta's hands into her own. 'Tell me what happened.'

Meeta was hesitant to share her problems with Pinky and remained silent.

'Meeta, talk to me. I'm your elder sister. If you keep things to yourself like this, you will die.'

Meeta looked into Pinky's eyes and almost without realizing it, she began to talk. She told Pinky about her father, about how he had worked endlessly and yet had died a poor man who was under a lot of debt, and how his debtors were eyeing not just her money but also her body.

'Listen to me carefully, Meeta. This world is cruel and the only way to survive in it is to become cruel yourself.'

'But, you are not cruel, and the world has been so nice to you.'

'What do you know about me, Meeta? You know nothing about me. You know nothing about my struggles and my pains. What you see is a lie, but it is a lie that has made me comfortable.'

'What do you mean?' That Pinky was once in a mess piqued Meeta's interest.

'Before I answer you, do you want to know why I like you so much?'

Meeta nodded.

'Because I was just like you. Naïve, simple, broken.'

Meeta waited for her to continue.

'Then I got smarter. I learnt how to cry for five minutes to enjoy the rest of the twenty-four hours. Meeta,' Pinky took a deep breath and continued, 'I'm a call girl.'

'What?' Meeta stood up. She was shocked. This simple friend of hers, for whom she had so much respect, was saying she was a prostitute.

'I knew you would be shocked. But to tell you the truth, I'm happy. I have money, quite a bit of it. This job at the parlour is just a front so that my relatives and neighbours don't doubt me. I have told them that I am a part-owner here.'

They sat in silence for a few minutes. Pinky got up and ordered two coffees.

After the coffee arrived and both had taken a sip, Pinky said, 'I have a list of ten clients. I work only with them. They are all in love with me.' She laughed.

'But don't they know each other?'

'Of course not, these are rich middle-aged businessmen who are bored with their wives. They take me with them when they travel and give me as much money as I ask for.'

'But don't you think what you are doing is immoral? You are making them cheat on their wives.'

'Those men, who snatched the money from you and said it didn't count for anything, were they not cheating? But let me answer your question. If I stop seeing them, they will find someone else.'

'But . . .'

'The best thing is, since they are not criminals, just simple family men, they are discreet, gentle and treat me well.'

Meeta gave her a tiny smile. She shifted in her chair and took a gulp of coffee. 'Tell me the truth—do you like going out with them?'

Pinky nodded. 'But I like the twenty thousand they give me after a weekend spent with them even more.'

'They give you twenty thousand? How much do you make in a month, Pinky?'

'Around one lakh, give or take. The best thing is no one in my family knows about it. And the men who give me the money are so scared about being found out that they protect this information with their lives.'

That night Meeta couldn't sleep. She was faced with a conflict. Even though Pinky had not said anything about Meeta getting involved in what she did, Meeta knew that if she asked, Pinky would help her.

Meeta would be seventeen the following month. She was a virgin and was worried about the train of thoughts that the conversation with Pinky had set rolling in her mind. What attracted her was the money and anonymity.

It was on Friday that Meeta declared to Pinky, 'I'm ready for it too. Will you help me?'

Pinky smiled. 'Of course.'

After the parlour closed that day, Pinky took Meeta along and bought her a few dresses and a nightgown. As she presented the clothes to Meeta, she said, 'Remember, you should always look good. Here is a small gift from my side.'

The next day, as instructed by Pinky, Meeta waited at a particular traffic light not far from the parlour. As she stood there, her small suitcase by her side, a car stopped next to her. It was a big one. The window rolled down and a man looked at her.

'Meeta?'

She nodded and got inside without a word. The man extended his hand and she shook it.

'My name is Aman. Nice to meet you.'

This was business. It was give and take. Everything would be over the next morning. Since it was her first time, Meeta was a little scared. But Pinky had briefed her on what to expect, so she was prepared.

She looked at Aman as he drove. He was handsome and Meeta feared that she would fall in love with him. She silently cursed herself for such an outrageous thought.

Aman didn't say anything. Soft music played in the car. After half an hour, the car rolled into the porch of a hotel. A man in a turban opened the passenger-side door and smiled at them.

Aman got out of the car and took her hand as she stepped out. She felt a shiver of electricity through her body. She walked by his side as they went up to the check-in desk.

This was the first time Meeta had entered a five-star hotel. Her head began to spin at the sight of all the flowers, mirrors and lights.

After Aman had checked them in, they took the lift. They were accompanied by a man who was carrying her suitcase. Aman had no luggage. The lift doors opened. They stepped out and walked down a long corridor, doors on both sides. Finally, they stopped before a door and the man accompanying them used an electronic key to let them in. He placed Meeta's suitcase on a rack, bowed and left.

Before she could say anything, Aman pulled her close. He started to kiss her and, within a few seconds, had removed all her clothes. Then he removed his own and pushed her on to the bed. It all happened so quickly that she didn't have the time to feel shy. Her senses had already been numbed by the opulence of the hotel and the fact that there would be a lot of money at the end of it. Her thoughts were all astray when Aman entered her.

She felt pain and cried out without wanting to, but Aman didn't stop. He went on and on, and slowly she began to relax. She looked at the man on top of her. His eyes were half-closed and he was ravaging her. He wasn't exactly gentle, but whatever he was doing, she soon began to enjoy it.

It was over when his face turned red and he threw his head back, letting out a weird cry. She felt wet inside. Then he rolled over to one side and all Meeta could see was the ceiling.

A few minutes later, Aman stepped out to the balcony to smoke. Meeta got up. She had bled a little and there was a red stain in the middle of the bed sheet. She pulled the sheet off the bed and took it to the bathroom. There, after a bit of a struggle as she figured out how the taps worked and where the soap was, she washed the bed sheet.

Then she changed into a new dress and looked at her reflection in the mirror. Aman was still in the balcony. She could hear his muffled voice. He was probably talking on the phone.

'Meeta, the prostitute,' she whispered to her reflection and laughed. Then she opened her vanity case and prepared her face to look her best for her master, Aman.

Surprisingly, there was no pain now. More surprisingly, there was no guilt.

Aman walked back into the room and looked at her. 'You are mind-blowingly beautiful.'

He pulled her towards him again and began to kiss her. Within seconds he had removed her clothes and his own too. He pushed her on to the bed a second time. But this time, everything was slower.

He climbed on top of her, entered her and began to make love to her. It was gentle and went on for a long time before he exploded.

This time, after Meeta emerged from the bathroom in another new dress, he looked at her and said, 'Let's have some food, I am famished.'

So far he had been speaking only in English and Meeta was responding in English as well. It was six in the evening and he ordered tea and some snacks. He pulled her into his arms once more during the night before sleeping and twice the next day before they left the hotel around one in the afternoon.

After he stopped the car at the same traffic light where he had picked her up, he turned to Meeta and said, 'You are lovely. I hope we can meet again.'

She nodded and accepted the bundle of notes he gave her. Then she got out of the car and hailed an autorickshaw. When she reached home, the first place she went to was the bathroom. There, she took out the bundle and counted the money. Aman had given her Rs 25,000 even though Pinky had fixed the deal for Rs 20,000.

The next day Pinky whispered, 'What did you do, Meeta? He can't stop talking about you.'

'Nothing. I did nothing. And he gave me twenty-five.'

'Lucky you. But tell me, how do you feel? Take your time, there's no hurry. We can forget about this. Consider it to be a misadventure. Whatever you do now will be your own responsibility. Just remember, money is an addiction, so stay in your limits.'

But Meeta's mind was elsewhere. She had earned Rs 25,000, the equivalent of five months' salary, in just one night.

Over the next three years, Meeta slept with many men. By the time she turned twenty, she had over fifty regular clients. She had paid off the debt and bought two cars: a Maruti Alto and a Wagon R.

By then, her mother knew what Meeta was up to. But she never said anything. Every time she gave her mother a bundle of notes for safekeeping, all Meeta said was, 'This is my share from the parlour.'

One afternoon, Meeta got a call from a man who identified himself as Sanjay. He said he had got her number from one of her trusted clients.

'I want to meet you in the evening.' He gave her the address.

Meeta met Sanjay in a hotel and, before she knew it, started to like him. He was different. He made her laugh and said things that she had never heard before.

The next morning, he pulled her close and looked into her eyes. 'I love you, Meeta. I would like to marry you.'

It had happened too fast, just in a few hours, and she didn't know what to say. Her heart wanted to say 'yes' as this was the first time a client had offered her marriage. Until that moment she had thought that marriage was out of the question for someone like her.

Finally, she said, 'I will let you know my answer soon.'

He seemed unprepared for this response but said nothing.

Meeta met him again the next day and then the day after that. He wanted to spend every night with her.

Meeta soon learnt that Sanjay was a car thief who was also involved in a few murders. He worked for a don based in Uttar Pradesh, whose gang members operated in Delhi, UP and Haryana.

Even though he was a criminal, for Meeta he was a kind man who seemed to love her a lot. Every time they met, he would give her flowers and gifts. None of her clients had ever given her flowers. A few did bring her gifts, but the flowers were new.

Sanjay kept pestering her for an answer to his proposal. Finally, Meeta realized that she had fallen for Sanjay, and one evening, just after a session of lovemaking, she said 'yes'.

They were in a hotel room and Sanjay ordered the most expensive wine on the menu. By now Meeta had started to smoke, do drugs occasionally and drink alcohol too.

'You are just mine now,' claimed Sanjay that night.

'Yes, just yours. I am putting an end to this business.'

Meeta changed her mobile number and stopped meeting men. Sanjay started transferring money into her account every month. It was more than what she had been earning. After four months of courtship, they got married.

Meeta's family was very happy. It was a simple ceremony. Her mother had booked a modest banquet hall and invited their friends and relatives. Pinky helped her buy her wedding dress and did her bridal make-up.

After the wedding, the two went to Kashmir for their honeymoon. Sanjay told her that he wanted to take her to Switzerland, but he didn't have a passport and because of the police cases against him, he would never be able to get one. Nonetheless, for the two of them, the honeymoon was pure bliss. Their love intensified and they had the time of their lives.

A month after their return, Meeta realized that she was pregnant. She called Sanjay and informed him. He was over the moon and said he would come home soon to meet her. Sanjay was in hiding at the time because of a crime that he had committed soon after they got married.

One week later, she received a call from Sanjay's friend Rohit. Meeta had met Rohit a few times and she knew that he was a close friend of her husband. But what he said sucked the breath out of her lungs. He said, 'Meeta ji, I am very sorry to inform you that Sanjay was killed last night in a police encounter.'

Meeta was devastated. The man she loved so dearly, the father of their yet-to-be-born child, had been snatched away from her. Unable to take the news, she left her home and moved to a hotel, where all she did was cry. Soon, she was back on drugs and stopped taking calls.

About a week after Sanjay's death, Rohit tracked her down. When she opened the door to a knock, Meeta found her mother and Rohit standing there. They took her home.

After Rohit left that night, Meeta's mother caught her swallowing some pills.

'What's that?'

'Nothing.'

'Are you out of your mind, Meeta? You are pregnant. The unborn child will be affected by this.'

Mother and daughter had a big fight that night. The next eight months, till the time of the birth of her son, were tough. On the one hand she felt sick all the time, whereas on the other, she couldn't stay away from the blue pills. Her mother helped her keep her sanity and stayed with her every minute of the day. Rohit visited them often and provided much-needed emotional support. But despite all these efforts, she missed Sanjay a lot. It was as if the world had cruelly taken away a vital body part.

Meeta started to hate the police. Rohit had told her that it was not an encounter but the police's brutality in broad daylight that had killed Sanjay. They could have arrested her husband, but they decided to kill him and then fabricated the story about an encounter.

When her son was born, her mother suggested that they call him Geet. Meeta agreed. But she could not breastfeed her own child. Her emotional turmoil and dependence on drugs had played havoc with her body.

One day, out of the blue, Rohit proposed to her. She was taken aback and looked at him with surprise. But what she saw was honesty and commitment. After thinking about it for a few minutes, she said 'yes'. The two were married soon.

But to her horror, Rohit too was killed by the police within weeks of marrying her.

After Rohit's death, Meeta started her business again. She got in touch with her old clients and they were happy to shower their love and money on her again. But this time, she took a bold decision. She rented a flat in New Delhi's Nizamuddin.

Rohit had a brother, Ashwini, who had sometimes accompanied him to Meeta's house. Meeta could tell that he liked her. And sure enough, a few months after Rohit's death, Ashwini proposed to her.

But this time she was in no hurry. There was a lot going on in her mind. Not only had her greed for money multiplied, but her dependence on drugs had blunted her emotions. All she wanted now was money. Lots of money.

With Ashwini's help, she recruited a few girls, housing them in the flat she had rented. These girls were uneducated and earned very little money in the Paharganj and G.B. Road areas where they worked as prostitutes. Meeta was able to convince a few decent-looking girls to work for her.

She taught them a few simple sentences in English, trained them on how to use cosmetics and bought them pretty dresses. Within a week, the girls could pass off as belonging to good families. Meeta had turned prostitutes into sophisticated call girls.

This brought her huge rewards. She paid the girls a monthly salary but sent them to clients every day, sometimes many times each day, depending on the demand. The girls didn't complain because they were now making twice of what they made in dingy Paharganj and were living in a decent flat where a cook and a caretaker took good care of them.

After a few months, Meeta's thoughts turned to Ashwini's proposal. Working closely with him, she had started to like him a lot and wanted to say 'yes'.

After one rather good day of business, Ashwini asked her again, 'Will you marry me, Meeta?'

She smiled and hugged him. 'Yes.'

This time, the marriage ceremony was sans any fanfare. The two were married quietly in a small temple outside Delhi. They moved into the flat adjoining the one where Meeta housed her girls.

Her business flourished. She herself had given up being a call girl before she had married Ashwini, and her job was now easier. One of her cars ferried the girls to a location of the client's choice. She sent the girl with a driver and one more male member of her gang whose job was to collect the money from the client in advance. The car would then bring the girl back to the flat.

Within a few months, Meeta had enough money to buy the flat she was living in, and she bought it in her mother's name. Geet, her son, was now living with her mother and she made sure that she met him once a week. She bought him toys and took him for movies.

One day, she received a call.

'Meeta didi?'

'Who is this?'

'I'm from Ashwini's gang. I'm sorry to inform you that Ashwini was killed this morning in a police encounter.'

Once again, Meeta was shattered. Just when things had started to get back to normal, the police had once again stolen the man she loved. She locked herself in her flat to grieve.

For days, the business was run by her cook, Vikas Sharma, who had been working with her for a few years. He took over as the manager and hired another cook while Meeta remained behind closed doors.

But she was back on track after a few weeks. This time, though, she decided to change her name. It happened quite by accident when an unknown number flashed on the screen of her mobile. The year was 2006 and she was in her flat in Nizamuddin.

'Hello?'

'I want to speak to Meeta,' said a male voice she had never heard before.

'Meeta is dead.'

'Oh?'

'What do you want?'

'I want a girl. Who am I speaking to?'

'Monu.'

She used to call Ashwini 'Monu'.

'Monu?'

She understood the man's confusion. Monu was typically a man's name.

She looked at the television, which was tuned to a Punjabi channel. A Punjabi song was playing. Across the screen flashed the word 'pataka'. An attractive girl was dancing to a solo number.

'Monu Pataka.'

This name became her new identity. Taking on her husband's name was her way of staying close to him.

Monu took to new drugs and her addiction fuelled her desire to further expand the business. She hired a few pimps and assigned them areas to operate in.

As her revenues rose, her list of girls also started to expand. Soon, she acquired a property in Saket as well.

By now, the police had learnt about her activities. As she began to expand, it started to get difficult for the junior policemen who were taking a cut from her to look the other way.

In 2007, therefore, she was in for a rude shock when she was arrested during a police raid. It took her a few weeks to get out on bail, but in 2008, she was arrested again.

The second time she was arrested she knew exactly what to expect and was not worried. Her lawyer was successful in getting her out on bail within days. But neither the lawyer nor her team saw the game the police was playing. They therefore didn't know that since she had been arrested twice for the same offence—violation of the Immoral Traffic Prevention Act, 1956—another arrest would put her in serious trouble.

In 2009, unaware of the danger she was in, Monu, in a shrewd power play, passed on information about her competitors Sachhawala Baba and Noori to the police. As soon as they were arrested, she took over their girls. Her operations were now no longer limited to Delhi and the surrounding areas but also spread to Kolkata, Mumbai and Bangalore.

It was 2011 and the cricket world cup was in full swing. Vikas Sharma came to her one morning.

'Monu madam, business has peaked. Most girls are working eight clients per day.'

'That's good.'

'Tomorrow is the final between India and Sri Lanka in Mumbai, and I think the demand will exceed what we can supply.'

Monu looked up from the line of cocaine that she was about to snort. 'So get more girls.'

He left. Around eleven, Vikas called her.

'Monu ji, I am with two customers. I had taken two girls with me, but they are not happy with them and want to see more.' He lowered his voice and added, 'They are ready to give us extra for this change of heart. Double rate.'

'Get them here and let them select. We are known to treat our clients as supreme, aren't we?'

Neither Monu nor Vikas had any idea that the two customers, who had selected the girls based on a WhatsApp conversation, were actually policemen in disguise.

The 'customers' were driven to the flat in Nizamuddin where there were more girls. They were made to sit in the drawing room and the girls were lined up in front of them. There were ten girls, all wearing designer clothes, and they all looked well-to-do and educated. None of them looked like the typical, garishly made-up prostitutes that one saw in the movies.

The two policemen, Srikant and Ram, knew they had to be careful. Their operation had gone smoothly so far. They had acted on a tip-off, established communication with Monu's service, and got this far on the pretext of paying more for the girls of their choice. As they looked at the girls and at each other, the bedroom door opened and a woman walked out. She was wearing jeans and a top. She looked at them and smiled.

Since one of them, Ram Singh, had arrested Monu before, he recognized her instantly, but Monu did not. He excused himself and stepped out. Once outside, he called his team, which was waiting in the vicinity.

Within a few minutes, the police team reached the flat and took everyone into custody. Their prize catch was Monu Pataka, and since she had been arrested for the same crime twice before, they could now impose the stringent Maharashtra Control of Organized Crime Act (MCOCA).

MCOCA had been implemented in Delhi by the home ministry in 2009. Under MCOCA, the statements recorded in a police station were admissible in the court, which wasn't the case earlier. Criminals would record their confessional statements in the police station but would change their mind in the court after meeting their lawyers. The MCOCA, therefore, gave more teeth to the police.

Monu was questioned and, since she didn't know the provisions of MCOCA, gave the police all the information they asked for. She accepted that she had been running the flesh trade business for a long time.

As soon as she learnt about MCOCA and her lawyer explained the implications of the statements she had made to the police, she was devastated. She was also addicted to cocaine and, within days, locked in jail, she started to experience withdrawal symptoms.

Sure that this was the end for her, she had no desire to spend her life in jail. The police had killed all the men she had loved and now they had destroyed her business and cornered her like a rat. Monu decided to kill herself. Suicide was the only solution. She tried swallowing all the sleeping pills that she had on her, but when that didn't work, Monu tried to hang herself from the ceiling fan in her cell using her chunni.

The duty constable heard the commotion and saved her. Monu was taken to the hospital, but she refused treatment. The doctors recommended psychiatric help, after which she was brought back to jail.

The case against Monu went to trial, but even after several months, the police couldn't prove the charge of organized crime due to a legal technicality. Yes, they did have a confessional statement, but the Act's application was for organized crime and the police could not prove this because of two reasons. For one, Monu did not have any property in her name, so technically, she was penniless. And for another, since she operated alone, there was no question of running an organization with other criminals. The charge sheet, which the police thought was watertight, did not stand up to the scrutiny of the law and, in 2014, the judge acquitted Monu for lack of evidence. It was a major setback for the police, but it was a huge relief for Monu who was convinced that her days were numbered.

Her acquittal came as a blow to the Delhi Police because they had spent considerable time and effort to arrest Monu and curb the illegal flesh trade. They were now more desperate than ever to punish her. Soon, they got the opportunity that they were looking for.

Since none of the girls who had been arrested with Monu had complained against her, the police desperately wanted someone to lodge an official complaint against her. It happened soon enough.

In 2014, a girl walked into a police station in Najafgarh, a locality near Delhi's western border with Haryana. It was 6 p.m. The girl was weak and appeared dehydrated. A constable saw her staggering in and, taking one look at her, knew that she was in trouble. He took her straight to the duty officer.

The girl was given water and after she had stabilized, she said, 'I've not eaten for the last five days. Can you give me food?'

The duty officer asked the constable to get her some juice and biscuits, which she ate quietly.

After she finished eating, the girl told the duty officer her story. 'Since I was twelve years old I have been sold to twelve different men. I've now run away from a man who was holding me in Rohtak. I took the first bus that I could.'

She paused several times as she spoke, due to weakness. Then she mentioned one name that made the duty officer sit up and listen carefully. The name was Monu Pataka.

'Sir, I was bought by Monu Pataka for one lakh rupees in 2009. She is an evil woman. She turned me into a prostitute. When I refused to do what she wanted me to, she kept me hungry for days. And when that didn't work, she made me a drug addict. She used to send me to men after giving me drugs. I felt so weak that I could hardly walk and didn't know what was happening to me. Her men would take me in a car and bring me back after I was raped by someone. I cried, pleaded, but she didn't listen to me. Finally, she sold me to a man in Lucknow.'

'Do you know where she lives?'

'Yes.'

'Will you be ready to file a complaint against her? That will give us reason to arrest her. Without a complaint from someone we can't do anything.'

'Yes, she is a bitch. I will file a complaint.'

The duty officer then asked her to accompany him to the hospital but she refused, saying that she would return the following day to sign her statement.

As the constable escorted the girl outside, the duty officer reached for the phone to call a senior officer. Getting Monu Pataka was high on the agenda of the Delhi Police. The humiliation of not being able to get her convicted despite MCOCA and a foolproof charge sheet was still fresh in their memory.

But the girl didn't return to the police station the following day. This was a setback.

A new police commissioner had recently been appointed for Delhi, and he had ordered a crackdown on the flesh trade. In accordance with this directive, a special team of two inspectors was formed to search for the girl. For several months, the two searched every place they suspected such a battered girl would hide in, but they couldn't find her. Just as they were contemplating filing an 'untraceable' report and closing the case, an inspector from the technical surveillance group reached out to them with good news.

'We have traced the number of one of her friends.'

The police was soon at the door of the girl's friend. She told them where they could find their target. They picked up the girl the same day, but she refused to cooperate.

'Why are you not cooperating with us?'

'Sir, I can't.'

'But you yourself walked into a police station in Najafgarh. Then what happened? Why have you been hiding from us?'

The girl began to cry and between sobs said, 'Sir, they will kill me if they come to know that I was the one who filed a complaint against that woman.'

It took the police several days of counselling to convince the girl that she was safe. Finally, she agreed to file a complaint and her statement was recorded in front of a magistrate. This was enough.

Monu Pataka was once again arrested in December 2017. This time she was charged under the Protection of Children from Sexual Offences Act, 2012, for forcing a minor girl into the flesh trade.

The case continued for a few months, but Monu was successful in getting bail. After her release from Tihar Jail in Delhi, she returned to her home where her new boyfriend welcomed her.

Monu was back in business, this time as an aggregator, someone who didn't keep any girls but worked only on commission.

Even though she has been in and out of jail since, her business has continued to grow thanks to a proficient tech team that kept her activities mostly anonymous.

Interesting fact: All the men Meeta, aka Monu Pataka, claimed to have fallen in love with were killed by the police. According to experts, she was the one responsible for these deaths. Using her cunning mind and charming ways, she successfully moved from one man to another. Men, who fell for her looks, told her secrets and details of their next crime, information that she used at will whenever she got bored with a man. Though this is what most people believe, a few say it is not entirely convincing and the killings might have been a coincidence.

3

The Lady Don of Delhi

'Why don't you earn some money?' Resham pleaded with her husband, Malkeet Singh.

Malkeet looked at her, his face blank. An uneducated man who hailed from Jodhpur in Rajasthan, he and his wife Resham had been living in Delhi for two years.

'Answer me! For how long can we live like this?'

Without a change in his expression, he said, 'I only know how to rear goats, Resham.'

'But this is Delhi, not your village. Where will you take the goats for grazing?'

Malkeet had no answer.

The couple had shifted to Delhi in 1985, right after getting married. Living in a temporary hut in the Govindpuri slums, they were finding it difficult to make ends meet. While Resham had worked as a maid, Malkeet washed utensils at a dhaba located on the edge of the slums. The arrangement had worked for a while, but then Resham got pregnant and found it difficult to keep her job.

Malkeet knew he had to do something or they would not have enough to eat. His wife needed healthy food and, therefore, in spite of his limited way with words, he started to ask the few people he knew in the area for advice and help.

One day, a man told him, 'Malkeet, why don't you shift to Sargam Vihar? Next to it is a small jungle where your goats can graze.'

'But I have no goats.'

'I know, but you once said that you wanted to raise goats, didn't you?'

Malkeet nodded, but his expression remained blank.

The same day, he went to see the place for himself. It was in south Delhi and right next to it, just as the man had said, was a jungle. He walked into the jungle and found it full of grass and trees. It was August and the monsoon that year, in 1987, had been kind.

Malkeet raised his hands and shouted loudly. For the first time since moving to Delhi and living in that stinking slum was he seeing so much greenery. There were no people around and since Malkeet was not the social kinds, he experienced a calmness and relief that he had almost forgotten after moving to Delhi.

He returned to Govindpuri and said to his pregnant wife, 'I have found a beautiful place in Delhi. Let's shift there.'

He explained his plan to erect a makeshift hut in Sargam Vihar and keep a few goats.

Resham didn't find the idea appealing. 'Are you out of your mind? We have come to Delhi to make a life, not herd goats and sheep. This we could have done in Jodhpur.'

'But that way, I will be able to earn some money.'

She looked at him and didn't say anything. The fact was that Resham liked him very much. His innocence and simple ways appealed to her. Malkeet never hung out with other men, drinking or gambling. He also didn't eye other women, like some others in the slums did.

She smiled and relented. 'Okay.'

The two of them shifted to Sargam Vihar the next morning. Malkeet spent the entire day hastily gathering bricks and stones, and erecting a tarpaulin over them. Resham busied herself with making a *chulha* with stones right outside the hut. By sundown, they had a small hut, sufficient for them to squeeze into, and an open kitchen right outside.

When they slept that night, they heard wild dogs and hyenas. Malkeet smiled in his sleep while Resham kept her eyes open, worried that a wild animal might attack them.

The next day, Malkeet got up early, cut firewood from the trees nearby, and said, 'I am leaving for Jodhpur now.'

'When will you return?'

He shoved his hand into the pocket of the kurta he was wearing and took out the few currency notes and coins he had. 'Keep this money. I will be back in three days.'

The previous evening, he had bought some atta and dal from a shop that was about a kilometre away from his new hut. Malkeet was confident that his wife would be able to survive for three days without him by her side.

After he left, Resham emerged from the hut and started to explore the area. It was difficult for her to walk, but the desire to find out more about their new neighbourhood got the better of her. There were a few huts like theirs, but all of them were far apart.

When she returned to her hut about an hour later, she took out the big knife that she had owned since her wedding day. She had bought it in Agra, where she was from, a day before her wedding and kept it with her at all times.

The knife was ten inches long and its width tapered to a point so sharp that if Resham aimed it at the ground, it would pierce through it and remain upright, balanced vertically. The cutting edge of the blade was razor-sharp and it had a dark wooden handle.

'Please be careful with this knife. It is a weapon to kill. Use it only in self-defence,' the seller had told her.

Over the next three days, Resham tried to speak to the people in the vicinity, but all the women kept to themselves and the men were never around during the day. They probably went to work, she imagined.

Nothing untoward happened while Malkeet was away. But when her husband didn't return on the fourth day, she began to get worried.

On the fifth morning, Malkeet returned. He was escorting a herd of ten goats and there was a big smile on his face. She smiled back.

Over the next few months, their life started to come back on track. Every morning, Malkeet took the goats to the jungle and brought them back in the evening. After this, he milked them and sold the milk.

The couple was happy. But within a few months of giving birth to their first child, Resham realized that she was pregnant again. Over the next five years, she had four children. The expansion of their family meant a greater burden on their resources.

She knew her husband couldn't earn more than he already was. This meant she would have to do something. But as a young mother with four children at home, all of them under five, it was not possible for her to get a regular job.

Since her husband was away from sunrise to sunset, she couldn't even leave the house. This made Resham irritable.

One afternoon, a voice called out to her from outside the hut.

As soon as she emerged, she saw a man standing there. His eyes were red and he seemed to be drunk. 'Help me! I want whisky.'

'Go to the whisky shop then. Why are you here?'

'Today is second of October; it's a dry day because it is Gandhiji's birthday.' He laughed and added, 'Don't act like you don't know. Now go inside and bring me my whisky. I will pay double.'

'I don't have any whisky.'

'I will pay four times.'

The man was not ready to believe that Resham didn't have whisky inside the hut. Her sharp mind started to work. She told him to come back after ten minutes. As soon as he left, she locked her hut, ran to a neighbouring hut and asked, 'Whisky?'

The woman gave her a bottle and asked for Rs 100.

'I will bring the money in five minutes.'

Before the woman could object, Resham ran back to her house. She opened the door and was relieved to find her children playing peacefully.

Soon, the man returned.

She came out, waved the bottle at him and said, 'Two hundred.'

He gave her the money and vanished with a gleeful smile.

Resham then ran back to the neighbouring hut and gave the woman Rs 100.

'My name is Mumtaz,' the woman said, 'Mumtaz Mahal.'

'And my name is Resham, Resham Jhopadi.'

The woman laughed. 'As you can see, I am also in a jhopadi like yours. I think I should change my name to Mumtaz Jhopadi.'

It was now Resham's turn to laugh.

After she returned to her hut, Resham realized that the man who had bought the whisky from her had probably been looking for Mumtaz's house. Thanks to his mistake, she had become richer by Rs 100 in just a few minutes.

She immediately made a list of dry days in Delhi and decided to stock up on whisky. Mumtaz told her that since the demand was more than the supply, she would be happy to help Resham out.

'Not just dry days, people are always looking for liquor after the shops pull their shutters down at eight in the evening. And during festivals, the demand peaks.'

Resham discussed her idea with Malkeet, but he didn't share her excitement. All he did was nod, just as he did whenever one of his goats made too much noise.

Resham borrowed Rs 2000 from Mumtaz at 2 per cent interest per month and bought liquor with the money. In just two months, she had sold everything and returned the money to Mumtaz. She now had Rs 1000 as capital. She bought some more liquor and, by the end of that year, by reinvesting month after month, she had earned Rs 10,000.

Her illegal business brought her family financial respite and they could now afford three proper meals a day, even buying fruits and sweets occasionally. However, a few competitors had sprung up in the area.

One of these was Mumtaz.

One day, Mumtaz and her husband came to Resham's hut and, standing outside, started to abuse her for taking away their business.

They created so much noise that a few people from the neighbourhood gathered and supported them. By the time Resham emerged from her hut, around fifty people had surrounded her house and were convinced that she was wrong.

'Stop!' Resham shouted.

This only emboldened the crowd and they insisted that either Resham move away from Sargam Vihar or shut down her liquor business.

Resham tried to reason with them. Her voice level, she said, 'Look, I started with Mumtaz's help. Now I can't be told to leave just when I have become dependent on this money.'

Mumtaz shouted back, 'I thought you wanted to make *some* money! But what you have done is taken the business away from us. We are penniless!'

Resham kept her cool, her eyes shifting from person to person in the crowd. 'I'm not the only one selling whisky in Sargam Vihar. There are other people who started selling after I did. Why don't you ask them to stop?'

Mumtaz's husband stepped up and slapped Resham.

This was too much for Resham. No one had seen it, but she had been hiding her knife behind her back all this while. She had brought it with her because the noise outside had frightened her.

Angry, she swung the knife in reflex. It sliced neatly through the man's jugular vein and he fell to the ground, screaming in pain. The crowd hovered over him.

Resham was taken aback. She rushed into her hut, gathered her children around and waited, her eyes on the door and the knife in one hand.

Within fifteen minutes, the noise outside subsided. The crowd had dispersed. But she didn't have the courage to step out and check. Resham had never killed anyone and she was sure that it was not possible to kill someone with just one wild swing of a knife. The man was wounded and would be fine soon, she convinced herself.

Finally, around sunset, the door jerked open. She jumped to her feet, holding the knife out in front of her. It was Malkeet. The sight of him was a relief. She told him the whole story, sobbing all the while. The children, who had been quiet for the past three hours, finally began to fuss, cry and ask for food.

Malkeet said nothing. In response, after they had been quiet for a few minutes, he told Resham a story of his own, about how one of his goats had behaved that day in the jungle. It was a funny story and Resham laughed.

Then he said, 'Don't worry too much about the incident.'

Early next morning, two policemen arrived and arrested her. Malkeet was yet to leave for the jungle. He looked at her expressionless.

'What have I done?' she demanded.

'You are being arrested for murder.'

'Murder!'

She was taken to the police station where she pleaded, 'I have five children. Who will take care of them?'

Resham had no idea what it meant to be in police custody. She was not even convinced that Mumtaz's husband was dead. All she was worried about was her children.

That evening, she was released from jail. Someone had posted her bail. That someone was a man called Pappu. As they walked back to her hut from the Sargam Vihar police station, Pappu said, 'All the people in our area contributed to pay for your bail.'

She didn't understand why they would do that. She went blank.

By then, they were close to her hut and she saw that many people were standing along the lane leading up to it, their heads bowed.

'They are paying their respects to you for killing that bastard.'

Resham then learnt that Mumtaz's husband was a nuisance who fought with everyone and eyed other women. She was also told that Mumtaz had left the area. Resham felt sad for the woman. She didn't regret killing a bad person, but she felt bad about hurting his wife.

Without intending to, Resham became the leader of her locality. The murder brought her a lot of notoriety. Rumours about her knife began to circulate. Someone said it had been gifted to her by a Japanese monk and was in fact a samurai sword. Another claimed that Resham could slice through the neck of a buffalo with just one strike.

Initially, she didn't know of these rumours, but as they reached her ears, she smiled to herself and added a few interesting twists.

'If I throw it towards an airplane, it will come crashing down.'

The people laughed when they heard this, but they believed every word of it. It was, after all, a knife with special powers.

Over the next decade, Resham's bootlegging business flourished. She made enough money to buy a large plot of land keeping her expanding family in mind. By 2001, Resham and Malkeet had produced eight children. While Malkeet kept to tending his goats, the children came under the tutelage of their mother. She taught them while they were young and soon they began to supervise the other activities that she now controlled.

As the unofficial leader of the locality, Resham spent a great deal of time sorting out the problems of the people in Sargam Vihar. One of the main bones of contention, she realized, was access to water.

One evening, a conversation with her son, Ramu, gave them an idea for a new business.

Ramu was thirteen. He wasn't interested in studies and had dropped out of school when he was in class three. He now worked full-time with his mother, buying liquor and selling it and managing the accounts.

'Beta Ramu, I am getting tired of this fight that the people have every day over water.'

'Mummy, but that's your job—to solve their problems. Everyone follows your decisions, so what's bothering you?'

'Why can't the Delhi Jal Board lay pipelines in our area to supply water? Just like in other parts of Delhi?'

'The problem is that our colony is not authorized, so they can't lay pipelines here. That's why the Delhi Jal Board has provided for three borewells in Sargam Vihar.'

'These borewells are the reason behind all the fights. I have to spend three to four hours every day sorting out issues of who got less and who got more.'

'Mummy, why don't we take over these borewells?'

'How can we do that?'

'Simple. We start supplying water to the people using a rickshaw so that they don't have to come to the borewells and the fights can stop.'

'But will the Delhi Jal Board staff agree?'

'We will charge the people for the water we supply to them and, from what we collect, we will pay the staff.'

That day, Resham decided to take over the borewells in the locality. While two of the staff attendants who were stationed at the borewells accepted Resham's offer without resistance, the third one had to be shown a pistol by Ramu. In addition to the knife that Resham owned, the family now had two pistols, both country-made and unlicensed. The man quickly agreed.

The residents agreed too. After all, they were getting peace of mind in return for a few hundred rupees. The facility of delivery to their doorsteps also appealed to them. At least, that was how Ramu put it to 'mummy', which is what everyone in the locality called her—all were willing to comply and were happy with the arrangement. But, in reality, no one had the courage to raise a voice against Resham.

Over the next few years, Resham and her eight sons became the water mafia in the region. Everyone dreaded them. Ramu was now twenty and his seven brothers were all over ten years of age. The family was large, but it was getting richer by the day thanks to their bootlegging and water business. And soon, more opportunities began to knock on Mummy's door.

Two of them made sense to Resham. One was extortion and the other was contract killing. Through her sons, she sent word out that she could get anyone bumped off provided she was paid the right fee.

The family was able to maintain its dominance in the region for a long time, but eventually, problems started to surface. Competitors from adjoining areas began to encroach on their territory and the sons realized that the only way to survive was to fight back. With this in mind, Resham's gang started to induct more youngsters.

But their competitors did not give up. Capitalizing on the fact that Resham's gang was uneducated, their rivals started to register cases against them. So although the family fought to retain its territory, along the way they got embroiled in many court cases.

By 2017, Resham and her sons had 113 cases of contract killing, extortion, murder, kidnapping for ransom, bootlegging and robbery registered against them. But instead of weakening the gang, this taught them crucial lessons about the Indian judicial system. They tried different lawyers until they found the best in the business, whom they then retained, paying them handsomely. As a result of this, in most cases, they were either granted bail or let off due to lack of evidence.

Resham and her family now lived in a two-storey fortress-like house. It had ten rooms, five on each floor. Mummy was sixty, a powerful don whom everybody dreaded. She had no fear: not of competitors, not of the police, not of the courts. Getting away with murder for so long had emboldened her.

One summer afternoon in 2017, a woman Resham knew asked to meet her. Her name was Shahnaz. One of Resham's sons escorted her into the room where Resham met people who needed her help.

'Mummy, I want help.'

'What do you need?'

'I want my stepson Wasim killed. He is eyeing my daughter and . . .'

'How much?' Resham interrupted her. She had no appetite for the woman's sob story.

'Sixty thousand.'

When Mummy nodded, Shahnaz handed her a photograph and told her where to find the boy.

'Advance?'

Shahnaz pulled out a bundle from her blouse and gave it to her. 'Thirty thousand. Rest, after the job is done.'

Resham waved her away. As soon as she left, Resham told her son, who had escorted Shahnaz inside and was waiting near the door, 'Call Ashok.'

Ramu and her second son, Rohit, were in jail at the time. Ashok was seventeen and this could be a good opportunity for him to learn the ropes.

When Ashok arrived, Resham said, 'Meet Janglee and tell him that if he kills the boy, Mummy will give him eighteen thousand rupees.'

Janglee was Ramu's best friend and part of Resham's extended gang.

'Yes, Mummy.'

Ashok was ecstatic. At last he was getting an opportunity to do what only the adults of the family were allowed to do. This would be his first kill. Till then, he had only sold alcohol and done a bit of robbery.

Around five that evening, Janglee and Ashok approached their target. Wasim had never seen them before as he lived in a different area. It was not easy, therefore, for Janglee to convince him to accompany them to the Sargam Vihar jungle for a party.

'Party? Why are you giving me a party?' Wasim seemed sceptical.

Janglee laughed an easy laugh. 'It will be fun. I think we can be good friends.'

'But I have never met you two before.'

'Are you afraid of drinking whisky with us?' said Ashok.

'No, I was just wondering . . . Anyway, let's go.'

They walked towards the jungle. Along the way, two of Ashok's brothers and two of Janglee's friends joined them. Janglee introduced them to Wasim.

They walked deep into the jungle and started to drink whisky.

Their target was just eighteen and had no idea what was in store for him. He was happy that he was being offered free whisky. There was chicken and paneer as well.

After about an hour, when Wasim was drunk, Janglee and the other five stood up.

Wasim tried to get up too but lost his balance and fell down. He tried a second time and this time he managed to stand up. His body, however, swayed.

Ashok was the first to kick him. He jumped in the air and kicked him on the jaw with his right foot. Wasim staggered and crashed to the ground, landing on his back.

It was now Janglee's turn. He kicked Wasim in the stomach. Wasim started to crawl away from them. By now he knew what was going to happen and he started to shout for help at the top of his voice. But they were deep in the woods and the jungle swallowed his screams.

As if they were playing a game, all six joined in. They kicked Wasim turn by turn for a long time. Eventually, when they got tired, they broke his neck. Then they sat down and finished the remaining whisky and food before deciding what to do next.

'We need to burn his face. That way no one will recognize this bastard,' said Janglee.

The other five nodded at these words of wisdom from their leader.

Once the boys had burnt Wasim's face beyond recognition, they threw the body into a bush and dispersed.

For the next two days, all was quiet. On the third day, the police started to conduct a search based on a missing person's report filed by the victim's father. The father had no idea that his own wife had paid for the murder.

Finally, two eyewitnesses came forward. They said that they had spotted the victim going towards the jungle with some boys. Since the police knew this was Mummy's area, they suspected her involvement. More resources were pressed into service in the hope that they would finally gather solid evidence against the woman don who had been ruling the area and creating havoc for its residents for the last three decades.

The police team questioned everyone living in the area, even children. Ultimately, their efforts paid off. A child, who was around ten, had seen Wasim being murdered. He had been hiding behind the bushes and was able to give the police a few names and descriptions.

The police found the body and sent it for an autopsy. The gruesome manner in which the young man had been killed rattled them and Janglee and his team were soon arrested. It took the police just a few hours to make Janglee open his mouth and point a finger at Resham.

The news of Janglee's arrest and his disclosing Resham's name reached her before the police did. Malkeet and she quickly left the house. It was time for her to go into hiding and seek anticipatory bail.

Resham had not expected such a response from the police. She was upset with Janglee for being careless enough to let people see him go into the jungle with the victim. But, above all, she was angry with him for taking her name. That was against their code of conduct and she would have to punish him.

Resham and Malkeet moved from city to city to evade arrest but kept in touch with their well-wishers to keep tabs on what was going on. When her lawyers informed her that it would not be possible to get anticipatory bail this time,

Resham was livid. She tried different lawyers, but all the bail applications were rejected. The police had charged her with MCOCA, which forbids the granting of bail.

Malkeet, over the past three decades, had never stopped tending his goats. He neither supported what Resham did, nor objected. Consequently, there was not a single case registered against him. As they moved from city to city, he kept her company as he always had. Even though he missed his goats and often wondered who was taking care of them, he didn't complain. They travelled to Allahabad, Lucknow, Bhopal and Kanpur.

As time went by, Resham's absence and the consequent lack of control started to hurt her business. While two of her sons were in jail, the others were unprotected and at home all by themselves. While two people, including Pappu, regularly visited her sons, Resham found the situation she and her family were in disturbing. She started to hear of others who had begun to creep into her area, which made her very angry.

At the police headquarters, however, the mood was upbeat. After years, they had succeeded in cornering the woman don.

The joint commissioner of crime (south) called a meeting of the six-member team that had been specially constituted to handle Resham's case.

'Though we have her cornered, I don't think she can be tricked easily. We need to do more,' he told them.

The team members remained silent, waiting for him to continue.

'We need to make her financially and psychologically weak. Write to the Delhi Jal Board today and ask them to take over the borewells in her area. Also, let's prepare a watertight case and get all her properties sealed.'

Although the police took these measures, Mummy remained out of the reach of the law. No one had any idea where she was. Even tracking her phone didn't help as she had started to use a new number as soon as she left her home.

After a few weeks, the joint commissioner reassembled his team. 'This is not working. The woman is tougher than we thought. But she is uneducated, let's not forget that. What use is our education if we can't outsmart her? I have an idea.'

There was pin-drop silence as everyone stared expectantly at the joint commissioner.

He took a deep breath, exhaled slowly, leant forward and said in a hushed voice, 'Let's spread a rumour that her house will be auctioned next Monday.'

Heads nodded slowly as the team realized that this would be the best course of action in the current circumstances.

When this piece of 'information' reached Resham, she was frightened. So far, all the appeals and anticipatory bail applications that her lawyers had filed on her behalf had failed. It was now time to get back into the ring and fight. Staying away and operating through the phone was not working. Missing his goats, Malkeet had stopped speaking altogether.

Back in Sargam Vihar, the police discreetly set the trap for Resham. They were confident that their ruse would flush her out. Policemen, dressed in plain clothes, stationed themselves near her house as inconspicuously as possible and waited. There was no moon at the time so they had to keep careful watch in the dark. It was also important for the team members to change their locations so that people didn't see the same person at the same spot for too long. From Wednesday till Sunday morning, there was no sign of Resham or her husband.

According to the rumour, the house was to be auctioned at 2 p.m. on Monday. The policemen had put up posters in the area informing the local residents of this great opportunity to buy a large house at a very cheap price.

Early on Sunday morning, around 3 a.m., a dog started to bark. Sub-inspector Sanjay Singh, who was pretending to be asleep on a cart, adjusted the blanket that was pulled up over his head to check the source of the sound. He spotted two shadows creeping forward. He remained in his position as the shadows stopped in front of Resham's gate and looked around.

Could these be Resham and Malkeet, he wondered.

Just then he saw the iron gates open. The two shadows disappeared into the compound. Yes, it was them. There was no doubt now, but he knew he had to move carefully. This was the most sensitive stage of the operation and he didn't want to take any hasty decisions. He slowly pulled his walkie-talkie close to his mouth and whispered, 'Target in sight. Approach ground zero.'

'Ground zero' was the code they had established for the house. He maintained his position for a few more minutes, but as he saw his colleagues approach the house from all directions, he threw the blanket aside and got up too.

Sanjay was the leader of the group. He signalled everyone to come closer. Once the team had formed a circle so tight that their heads touched, he spoke softly, 'Vicky and Tiger, you go to the back of the house and stay there. In case they try to escape from that side, chase them. Others, come with me.'

Sanjay knocked loudly on the metal gate and waited. Nothing happened. A light was switched on inside the house, but it was turned off almost immediately.

Sanjay used the loudhailer. 'Resham, come out, or we will come inside and arrest you.'

Nothing happened for a few minutes. Just as he was contemplating his next move, he noticed a figure walking towards the gate. It stopped halfway. Sanjay switched on his torch and the beam caught the figure of the sixty-two-year-old godmother.

She looked tired and older than her age. Being on the run for months had played havoc with her health. And now, finally outsmarted by the police, there she stood, defeated and helpless.

Resham was joined by another figure. Sanjay and his team saw Malkeet for the first time. Though they had a picture of Resham because of her involvement in so many cases, no one knew what Malkeet looked like. But the way he stood next to her, showing his allegiance, was quite a sight.

Sanjay switched off the torch. The darkness was blinding. But they were no longer worried that the culprits would try to flee.

As soon as the gates were opened Resham was taken into custody and driven away in a police jeep. Malkeet tried to run behind the jeep for a while but gave up in the end.

The following day, Sanjay met her in custody. 'Resham, the newspapers are saying that you are Delhi's first woman don. Are you a don?'

It was a light-hearted comment to get a reaction out of her. What Sanjay received in return was a response that only a hardened criminal could give. Resham looked at him, hard and long, before turning away to stare at the wall again. Her silence was her answer and the look, her weapon. While she might have looked like an unassuming old lady, the fire in her eyes showed him who she really was.

Interesting fact: The police found it difficult to arrest Resham's sons because every time they came to Sargam Vihar in response to a complaint about the petty crimes that they had committed, the children were never at home. The police tried showing up at different times of the day but they always got the same result. It was only in 2017, after the police found Wasim's body in the adjoining jungle, that they learnt the reason behind this. Resham's sons had made a few temporary shelters in the jungle where they could stay for as long as they needed to. They would stock up on food and water and stay there, undisturbed, for weeks. Or until the heat died down.

4

The Tinder Murder

A tired Laxman Sharma walked into his home in Jaipur after work one evening, but the sight of his two-year-old son, Krish, lifted his spirits. He smiled and picked him up. Krish flashed a toothy smile at his father and turned to look at his mother, Sunita, who stood in the doorway to the bedroom. Sitting in the living room, Laxman smiled at her too. Just then, his father, Bhuleshwar Prasad Sharma, walked into the room.

'*Arre*, beta, so late today. Don't work so hard!'

'Papa, I have only one life. I should work hard so that all of us can be happy and comfortable.'

Bhuleshwar walked up to his son, placed a hand on his shoulder affectionately and said with his eyes moist, 'Lucky beta, I have already lost two sons. I don't want anything to happen to you. Please don't overwork yourself. Have you ever thought what would happen to us if some harm were to come to you? Sunita, Krish and I, we don't have anyone else in this world.'

'Papa, don't worry, all is well. I will always keep your words in mind.'

Sunita went to the kitchen to prepare some adrak-wali chai, which Laxman enjoyed at the end of a long day. It was 7 p.m.

Married for three years, everything had been going well for them as a family. But recently, something had been bothering Sunita. Although she was sure that her husband loved her, his behaviour was worrying her. For the past few weeks, her husband had been preoccupied. One night, she woke up at 2 a.m. to find Laxman staring at the screen of his mobile phone. His expression, visible in the blue glow of the screen, was peculiar.

'Laxman, is all well?' she had asked.

He had appeared to be alarmed and his first reaction had been to hide the phone. Then he had mumbled, 'Nothing, it's just office work. You won't understand.'

She had turned away and closed her eyes. She knew she shouldn't assume anything, even though all sorts of thoughts started to take shape in her mind. She had placed her hand on little Krish's head and drifted off to sleep. But something had been stirred deep in her mind and she found herself awake after an hour. When she turned to look at her husband, he was fast asleep. She had then closed her eyes and mumbled a prayer for his safety. Mouthing the words 'I love you', she had smiled and gone back to sleep.

This evening too, his eyes looked at her, but it was as if he was looking right through her. By the time she brought the tea to the living room, Laxman had freshened up and was playing with Krish. Bhuleshwar was sitting on the sofa, reading a newspaper.

Seeing Sunita, Laxman got to his feet. He smiled at her before turning to his father. 'I have to go out for a few hours. It's for some work related to my business.'

Ignoring the tea, he dashed into the bedroom as Sunita and Bhuleshwar exchanged looks of confusion. Krish was too preoccupied with his toys to notice anything.

Laxman emerged from the bedroom ten minutes later, wearing his best clothes. He had applied cologne generously and his hair was slicked back with gel. It appeared as if he was going out for a party, not for work.

Five feet nine inches tall and of medium build, Laxman was an average-looking man. He was in the business of supplying building materials to small construction companies. But whatever business he was heading out for that evening was evidently different. Going by his clothes, it was clear that he was not on his way to meet contractors, supervisors or labourers, the kind of people he usually met in his line of work.

Laxman looked at his father. 'Papa, can I take your car? That way I will be able to return home sooner.'

'Of course. But where exactly are you going?'

'Thanks, papa, I am in a hurry, I will tell you after I return.'

Laxman drove towards Malviya Nagar, a posh residential locality in Jaipur. He admired himself in the mirror and smiled. He was on his way to meet his new girlfriend, Preeti Sethi, who lived alone in an apartment complex called Lake View Enclave. Laxman had met Preeti on Tinder a couple of months ago.

Laxman was a teetotaller, but he knew that Preeti liked alcohol. Besides, a few drinks would set the ball rolling. So he stopped at a wine shop en route. It was just before 8 p.m., and since wine shops in Jaipur close at that time he wanted to buy the alcohol quickly. He smiled at the prospect of what lay before him. Did he need a condom? Yes, he did. After buying an expensive bottle of Scotch, he walked to a pharmacy nearby and bought a packet of condoms. Kamasutra? Pack of three? No, he returned the box and asked for a pack of ten instead, a hungry smile on his face, his eyes twinkling.

Laxman continued on to Preeti's house. Since it was a hot May evening, stepping out of the car had made him sweat. He increased the fan speed of the air conditioner and began humming his favourite song as he negotiated through traffic.

Fifteen minutes later, Laxman was at Preeti's door, sex and a night of debauchery on his mind.

'Hi Vicky', Preeti opened the door and welcomed her boyfriend.

For her, his name was Vicky Bajaj. That was what Laxman called himself on Tinder. On his secret profile, only one thing was true and that was his picture. All other details, including his wealth, marital status and city of residence, were fabricated. On Tinder, Laxman Sharma was a rich businessman whose company had an annual turnover of over Rs 50 crore. He lived in Delhi and was unmarried.

Laxman tried to embrace Preeti. She stepped aside and laughed. 'Arre, jaldi kya hai [what's the hurry]! Let's talk for a while.' With this, she walked into the living room and Laxman followed her swaying hips. As she turned to look back at him, he held out the bottle of Scotch.

'This is for you, Preeti, for our love.'

She signalled with her eyes that he should keep it on the coffee table. After he did, she said, 'I'm having some trouble with my TV. Can you help me fix it?'

Laxman nodded. The TV was switched off. He walked up to it and bent down to check if it was plugged in. It wasn't. He smiled to himself and inserted the plug into the socket and flicked the TV on. Loud music instantly filled the room. It was so loud that he didn't hear anyone approaching from behind.

As he turned to ask Preeti for the remote, he came face-to-face with three people. One of them was Preeti. The other two were men he had never seen before. They were glaring at him with bloodshot eyes.

'Preeti, what . . .'

The two men pounced on him. Before he could move an inch, they had him firmly in their grip. They tied his hands and dragged him towards a bedroom. He could not even scream for help as his mouth was the first thing they had taped.

One of the men, his expression crazed, said in a loud voice, 'Chinta mat kar amirzaade, hum tujhe marenge nahin [Don't worry, rich man. We won't kill you].'

The second man added, 'Khali dus lakh rupye dilwa de [just get us Rs 10 lakh].'

Laxman looked at Preeti, who was standing right behind them. Her expression was unreadable. His first thought was that two unknown men had attacked Preeti and him. But Preeti hadn't been tied up, he saw.

Then Preeti spoke and Laxman realized that they were all in it together. 'Dekho, Vicky Bajaj. We wish you no harm, but we need money. Give us ten lakhs and we will let you go.'

Laxman tried to speak, but since his mouth was taped, he couldn't. Preeti stepped forward and pulled off the tape. Before he could utter a word, she hissed into his ear, 'If you shout, these men will kill you. They don't know what they are doing. They are high on cocaine.'

Restrained, out of choices and scared, Laxman nodded weakly. But nonetheless he was sure he would be able to talk the men out of whatever they had planned for him. He looked at them closely; they seemed barely out of college.

'I don't have ten lakhs.'

The three kidnappers were not convinced. For them he was Vicky Bajaj, a rich man from Delhi.

The first man slapped him so hard that Laxman's vision was blurred for a few seconds and his ears rang.

The men waited.

'I swear I don't have ten lakh rupees.'

The second man hit him this time. It was a punch straight on his nose. Blood oozed out and his eyes watered because of the pain. He felt the blood trickle down his lips and drip on to his expensive shirt.

'Search him,' Preeti ordered.

The two men started to go through his pockets. As they removed his wallet, a condom packet fell out. The three of them laughed hysterically and one of the men kicked it under the bed. The search also revealed his car keys, a driver's licence and an Aadhaar card.

Preeti picked up the card and frowned. 'Whose card is this? Who the fuck is Laxman Sharma? But this is your picture, Vicky.'

'My name is Laxman Sharma.'

'What? You sonofabitch! You lied to me. Now don't tell me you're not from Delhi.'

'I am not from Delhi. I'm really sorry for all the confusion.'

The kidnappers looked at one another. This was a roadblock. Their plan had been to extort money from a rich man by scaring him and then letting him go. They had assumed that he would not go to the police because he had an image to protect.

'Are you married?' Preeti wanted to know to what extent she had been tricked.

Preeti was twenty-seven years old and had cheated over a thousand unsuspecting men who had wanted to have sex with her. Her method was simple. Step one, befriend a man on Tinder. Step two, after a few emotional chats, invite the guy home, serve expensive Scotch and, finally, tell him that if he did not give her the money she demanded she would accuse him of trying to rape her. Without exception, everyone paid up. And no one had ever complained to the police.

There was another method that she used. Preeti had a website on which she posted fake profiles of attractive Indian women and advertised them as call girls. When someone contacted the phone number listed on the website, she would fix a meeting at a five-star hotel. She would then go to the hotel to meet the man. After introducing herself, she would take the agreed upon sum from the man, tell him that she needed to pay her driver and then run off with the money. Only once was she chased by a man who had given her Rs 20,000. He caught her and lodged a complaint with the police, but Preeti was released after she accused the man of rape.

Laxman raised his eyes to meet hers and said, 'Yes, I'm married.'

It was now Preeti's turn to slap him.

'You bastard, you lied to me! Do you have kids?'

'Yes. A son.'

Preeti looked at his Aadhaar card again and realized that the man was a resident of Jaipur.

The three abductors held a quick meeting.

Preeti looked at one of the men and asked, 'Dinesh, kya karein [what do we do]?'

Dinesh Kohli looked at Lovely Ahuja, the other man, his classmate from their college in Bikaner, and said, 'Darling, you tell us.'

Both Dinesh and Lovely were twenty years old. Dinesh was in love with Preeti and had been staying with her for the past few months. Lovely visited them sometimes. Preeti had met Dinesh through Tinder in April 2018. She liked him a lot as he seemed smart and fearless, unlike her previous boyfriends. The two were planning to get married and had even got each other's names tattooed on their arms.

At the moment, all three were high on cocaine.

'Okay, let's keep it simple. Let's call the bastard's father and ask for a ransom of ten lakhs. Once that is paid, we will let him go.'

Preeti looked at Laxman. 'What should I call you now, *harami*, Vicky or Laxman?'

Laxman avoided meeting her probing eyes. She kicked him but yelped in pain as her ankle twisted. She limped to a stool and sat down, her back against the wall. The men took over and started kicking and punching him. The exercise excited them and Laxman's cries of pain egged them on.

Preeti was beautiful and intelligent. She had grown up in Beawar, a city in Rajasthan. Her father was a professor at the government college there and her mother, a schoolteacher. She had done well in her class XII examinations and her parents wanted her to become a professor. They had sent her to Jaipur to join a college.

When Preeti arrived in Jaipur seven years ago, she shared a room with another woman. Jaipur had surprised her with its opulence. She immediately developed a liking for expensive things. It started with clothes, shoes and accessories. But soon she realized that she would never have the money to own the things she desired.

One day, her roommate introduced her to someone. She told Preeti that the man would help her get clients who would pay her a lot of money if she slept with them. Preeti agreed without hesitation. She needed money to buy the things she wanted but couldn't afford with the meagre allowance that her parents sent from Beawar. Within a year, she was arrested during a police raid but was able to get bail immediately. This emboldened her and thus began her career in crime and prostitution. Her father learnt about her first arrest and tried to talk her out of the path she was on but when he failed, he disowned Preeti.

After fifteen minutes of beating Laxman, Dinesh and Lovely finally got tired and stopped. Laxman's head lolled to one side and his expensive clothes were soaked in blood.

The three abductors went to the drawing room and sat around a table quietly, each thinking about what to do next. Preeti was the first to speak.

'Listen, this bastard needs to be punished. Let's call his father and ask for ransom. We will make him call. Once the money is transferred, we will kill him.'

'Kill him?' Lovely mumbled uncertainly.

'Saale, phat gayi na teri [Scared, aren't you]?' Dinesh glared at him.

Preeti butted in, 'Okay, don't fight now. One thing is clear—we can't let him go. He is from Jaipur and will certainly go to the police and we will be caught. Do you want that, Lovely?'

'No,' he mumbled weakly.

'Good.'

It was midnight by then. They decided to rest for a while. Preeti winked at Dinesh and they walked hand in hand to the bedroom. Lovely understood what that meant and he lay down on the sofa. Soon he could hear them from the other room. There was laughter, moaning and panting. He closed his eyes and tried to sleep, trying to shut out his surroundings. He woke up when somebody shook him. He opened his eyes and saw Dinesh. Preeti was right behind him.

'Saale, chutti manane aaya hai [Are you here on a holiday].'

'Chutti to tu mana raha hai, saale [you are the one who seems to be on holiday],' he retorted. When Dinesh understood what his friend meant, he looked at Preeti and they both laughed.

'You also want a girl, bhai?'

'Enough,' Preeti stepped in. 'We have work to do.'

The three opened the door of the room where they had left Laxman the previous night. He had slumped to the floor.

Preeti immediately wondered if he was dead. She went up to him.

Laxman heard footsteps approaching and straightened up, pushing his body against the wall. His hands and legs were still tied. One of his eyes was swollen shut and the other was partially open.

Preeti knelt down. 'Saale, tera naam kya hai [What's your name]?'

She asked the question in a sing-song voice and the two men behind her began to laugh.

Dinesh said, 'Lucky Bajaj hai mera naam.'

Lovely said, 'Nahi, Laxman Sharma hai mera naam.'

Preeti turned to look at the two of them and smiled. 'Iski biwi ghar pe hai and he wanted to fuck me. Bastard [Imagine, he has a wife at home]!'

In one swift motion she slapped him. Dried blood stuck to her palm.

'Yuck, dirty blood.'

While she was in the bathroom washing her hands, Dinesh picked up Laxman's phone and switched it on. They had turned it off the previous night, before they began hitting him.

Preeti returned to the room. 'Saale ko bol apne baap ko phone karega [ask him to call his father].'

'Number bata,' said Dinesh.

'Wait.' Preeti approached Laxman and spoke slowly, one word at a time, 'Apne. Baap. Ko. Bol. Tere. Account. Me. Das. Lakh. Daal. Dega. Ek. Ghante. Mein. Nahi. To.

Tu. Khallas [Ask your father to deposit Rs 10 lakh into your account in a hour. If he doesn't, we will kill you].'

After Laxman managed to blurt out the number, Dinesh dialled it and held the phone to Laxman's ear.

'Papa, inko das lakh de do aur muhje bacha lo [Please give them Rs 10 lakh and save me].'

Preeti pulled the phone away and put it to her ear. She heard a man's voice, 'Lucky beta, kya hua? Kahan ho tum? [Lucky, what happened? Where are you?]'

Preeti responded, 'Ten lakh rupees in your son's account if you want to see him alive.'

'I don't have ten lakhs.'

'How much can you deposit?'

'Two to three lakhs. Please don't hurt my son. I will arrange the rest of the money soon.'

'Tera beta kamina hai. Doosri auroton pe nazar daalta hai. Saale tum sab kamine ho [Your son is a rascal. He eyes other women. All of you are rascals].'

She hung up. She was breathing heavily. This man in front of her was a liability. He had no money, his father had no money, and now Preeti would not have the money she desperately needed to help her lover, Dinesh, pay off a debt of Rs 20 lakh that he had incurred during his days in Mumbai as an unsuccessful model and an actor.

They waited in silence and finally, after about an hour, when they received an SMS on Laxman's phone that Rs 3 lakh had been transferred to his account, they asked him for the PIN. A weak and tired Laxman mumbled his secret code with a request that if they let him go, he would never tell anyone about them.

'I can speak to some friends and get the rest of the money,' he pleaded.

As he told them names of his friends, Dinesh found their numbers in the contact list on Laxman's phone and called them. Each time he heard a 'hello', he pressed the phone to Laxman's ear. Laxman asked five friends for money. Each of them told him how much they could afford to loan at such short notice. Laxman told them he would meet them later in the day to collect the money.

'Kill him!' Preeti declared after the final call.

Dinesh didn't say anything. Lovely opened his mouth but shut it without a word as soon as he met Preeti's glare.

'Yeh jhutha aur makkar aadmi hai [He is a dishonest man]. Can you expect a man who isn't loyal to his own wife to be loyal to us? He will go to the police and we will be arrested. There is no choice. Kill this harami.'

She nodded at Dinesh. He approached Laxman, grabbed him by the throat and tried to strangle him. It was difficult for him to maintain his grip as Laxman, realizing the danger he was in, started to thrash about violently. Finally, with Lovely's help, Dinesh got Laxman on to the bed. They tied him up with more ropes so that he was unable to move even a millimetre. But even then, despite his best efforts, Dinesh was unable to kill him.

When Dinesh was tired, Lovely tried to kill Laxman. He picked up a pillow and tried to smother their victim. After a lot of effort, when the three of them saw Laxman go still, they presumed he was finally dead. But when they checked, he still had a pulse. Laxman had only lost consciousness.

Preeti opened a cupboard and took out a large knife. She handed it to Dinesh. By now Laxman, who was conscious, was again struggling to be free. While Lovely and Preeti held him down, Dinesh slit his throat. It took him more than five attempts, but finally the man was dead.

It was time for the next step. Preeti told the two men, 'If you act quickly and do exactly as I say, we will all be safe.'

Dinesh and Lovely, both seven years younger than Preeti, had clearly accepted her as the leader. They nodded in agreement.

'First, we need to get rid of the body. I'll go and withdraw money from this bastard's account and then get suitcases.'

Half an hour later, she returned with two large suitcases.

'Why two?' Dinesh asked her.

'Because we will stuff the body in one and carry the other one empty. Since we will return with a suitcase, the neighbours will not suspect us.'

The idea might have been stupid, but to their drugged minds it appeared to be a smart move. Almost immediately, however, they encountered their next major problem. Laxman was too big for the suitcase. They tried to fold his hands and legs but were unable to fit him into the suitcase. The next step was obvious. After over two hours, they managed to hack his body into parts, stuffed it into one of the suitcases and zipped it up. There was blood all over the bed sheet. The mattress had soaked up a lot of it too, but these things could be attended to later.

Preeti opened the door of her flat and looked around. It was 2 p.m. and there was no one in sight. She signalled her accomplices to follow. While Dinesh carried the suitcase with the body, Lovely pulled the empty suitcase. They got into Laxman's father's car and drove towards Amer, an area Preeti knew to be desolate and thus an ideal place to dispose the body of.

Dinesh was driving. Preeti was in the passenger seat in front while Lovely was in the back seat with the suitcase containing Laxman's body.

A while later, they got rid of the body and returned to Preeti's flat with the empty suitcase as planned.

After returning home, Preeti told the men that she had to meet someone in a five-star hotel. She quickly ate some bread and eggs, which Lovely had rustled up, and left in a cab, promising to return soon. On the way, she stopped at an ATM and withdrew Rs 20,000 from Laxman's account. At the hotel, she met a man who had contacted her through her escort services website, took Rs 20,000 from him and told him that she would be back after paying her driver. From the hotel, as always, she went back home.

By the time she returned, Lovely had left for his house and Dinesh had tidied up the mess. She looked at Dinesh as he held up his hand.

'What's that?'

'A new number plate.'

'That's smart! You're learning fast. So, where do we go?'

'First, I want you.'

The two hugged and kissed and walked hand in hand into the bedroom.

Unknown to Preeti, Dinesh and Lovely, Laxman's family had taken steps to find him after receiving the ransom call. While Laxman's father was busy trying to arrange the remaining Rs 7 lakh, Sunita had told her brother about the kidnapping, who then informed the police.

The team at Murlipura police station—the local thana where the first information report (FIR) had been registered—had made some progress in the case. They had successfully accessed the call log that had details of the people Laxman had contacted while he was held captive.

All of them told the police the same thing—that though Laxman had called them the previous day and asked for money, he hadn't turned up to collect it. One of Laxman's friends, Paresh, informed the police that Laxman was involved with a woman who lived in Lake View Enclave in Malviya Nagar. The police, who were monitoring Laxman's bank account, also learnt that a woman had withdrawn Rs 20,000 from an ATM using Laxman's card at a location not far from Malviya Nagar. Further, they had been able to determine that Laxman had called his friends from Lake View Enclave. The police were therefore sure of the location where Laxman had been kept. But before they could go there, someone informed them about a body that had been found in a suitcase on the outskirts of Jaipur.

While a team of two went to Lake View Enclave to keep watch, another team proceeded to Amer. There, they found the suitcase with the body parts stuffed inside. The remains were swollen and had become stiff. The police had to ultimately cut open the suitcase to get the body out. The hands and legs had been tied with a rope. There were no documents that could identify the dead person. Since no other

crime had been reported in the city, the police suspected that
this was Laxman Sharma's body.

They called Bhuleshwar Prasad Sharma and asked him
to come to the hospital to identify the body. Once the father
identified his son's body, the case took a dramatic turn. A
case of abduction had turned into murder. More resources
were mobilized and a crack team proceeded to Lake View
Enclave.

By the time the police reached Preeti's third-floor
flat, three hours had elapsed since the body had been
discovered. They arrested Preeti and Dinesh who were
about to flee from the house in Laxman's car. Upon being
questioned by the police, the owner of the house, who
had rented the flat to Preeti, informed them that she
had claimed to be a professional who made videos for
YouTube.

Lovely was arrested a few hours later.

In police custody, Preeti, Dinesh and Lovely confessed to
murdering Laxman.

The investigation continued for the next three months.
After speaking to forty-five witnesses and listing more than
100 pieces of evidence, the police finally filed a 400-page
charge sheet in the trial court on 30 July 2018 against Preeti
Sethi, her live-in partner, Dinesh Kohli, and their friend
Lovely Ahuja.

The speed with which the Jaipur police acted in this
investigation, their commitment and professionalism received
the praise it deserved.

Interesting fact: During an interview a few days after her arrest, on being asked about her methods of extorting money, Preeti Sethi reacted angrily on camera saying that in running off with the money given by the men who were seeking call girls, she was performing a social service. She expressed her sadness that now that she had been arrested, she would not be able to continue with this social service, which punishes those who seek pleasure in other women while their own wives wait for them at home.

5

An Actress and Her Two Lovers

As the plane started to taxi at the Bengaluru airport, Marie looked out of the window. It had just rained and the tarmac was shining in the late evening sun. When the plane landed in Mumbai two hours later, it would be dark.

Marie loved the dark. It gave her a chance to look glamorous and do things that were not possible during the day. Sometimes in Bengaluru, where she had worked in a few films and done several print and TV advertisements, she would wear her best dress, pair it with exotic heels, apply dark and glossy make-up, and go for a stroll. The way men looked at her gave her a high that no other experience ever could. She felt beautiful and sexy, like someone who was desired by dozens. It was this desire to attract men that had prompted her to take the bold step of moving from the Kannada film industry to Bollywood.

After take-off, Marie had glanced at the man seated next to her. He was in his sixties, fit for his age, and had the confidence of a rich man. She wondered if he worked in the film industry.

The plane had reached cruising altitude and the air hostesses began to wheel the food trolleys down the aisles. By then, Marie was certain that her neighbour was under the influence of her charm.

'Madam, good evening! What would you prefer, veg or non-veg?' asked the air hostess.

'Non-veg,' Marie said and immediately wondered if her companion was a vegetarian.

When the air hostess asked him the same question, he requested a vegetarian meal. This was Marie's window of opportunity to begin a conversation.

After the food was served, she turned towards her neighbour, placed one elbow on the edge of the tray table where her untouched food lay, and said sweetly, 'Sir, if my non-veg meal bothers you, I can exchange it for a veg plate.'

The man turned towards her. His eyes twinkled as he said, 'Oh, no, no! No problem, but thank you.'

In that split second, Marie sensed what would follow. She knew she would find out all about her companion in the next few minutes.

After the man had swallowed his first bite, he asked, 'To Mumbai for work?'

Marie continued to chew, taking her time to answer. 'I'm an actress. I'm relocating to Mumbai.'

'Actress? Wow, I should have guessed. You are, well, so . . . perfect, I mean attractive . . .'

'Thank you.'

The man's fumbling response and discomfited expression gave Marie more confidence. After they had finished their meals and were sipping their coffees, Marie once again turned to him. 'Do you live in Mumbai?'

'No, I live in New York. I work there. My flight leaves from Mumbai, which is why I'm going there.'

Marie was impressed because for her America meant Hollywood, where she dreamt of going some day. With her beauty and charm, and the fact that she was prepared to do anything to impress those who mattered, she knew her chances of success were high.

Nonetheless, she realized that this man was of no use to her. Had he been connected to the Mumbai film industry, she would have put her charm to further use. She finished her coffee and closed her eyes.

After the plane landed, Marie ignored the man's goodbye and walked into the arrival area. She paused for a second, looked around for the washroom and headed straight for it. The sight of herself in the mirror gave her a high. This was Marie, the future top heroine of Bollywood, she thought to herself as she gazed at her reflection.

She took her make-up kit out of her handbag and, after a close examination of her face, began to touch-up. Five minutes later, she stepped back, satisfied with her appearance.

Marie adjusted her short skirt and figure-hugging Lycra top, twirled in front of the mirror for a final look and then left the washroom, walking confidently towards the baggage carousel. She picked up her suitcase, ignored the men who were staring at her and walked out of the exit.

The hotel she had booked a room in had promised to send a taxi. She spotted her name on a placard held up by one of the several dozen drivers near the exit. As he took her suitcase, she walked behind him, an extra swing to her hips.

The taxi pulled up outside the hotel, which was located in Andheri. It was small, had a gaudy exterior, and when she walked in, a small reception area. The place was a disappointment. The pictures she had seen online had been impressive, but what she saw in reality was a one-star hotel masquerading as a three-star.

Once she was in her room, she lay on the bed, which was relatively clean. First, she had to call her fiancé. In fact, she was surprised that being the possessive man he was he had not called her yet.

'Hi, honey, I was about to call you. Have you reached? How is the hotel? Are you comfortable?'

Just as she had expected; John Varghese, her fiancé, didn't disappoint.

'Yes, honey, it's all good.'

John was a lieutenant in the navy. He was a year older than her and was currently posted in Kochi. They had met in Bengaluru two years ago when she was just starting out in the Kannada film industry. She liked him immensely. He was good-looking, intelligent, had a good sense of humour and was completely in love with her. He was so handsome that had he not been a naval officer, he could easily have been a star in the film industry.

As their romance reached new heights, so did her graph in the Kannada film industry. One evening, while they sat in the café of a five-star hotel looking out over the city as the sun set, John had gone down on one knee and said, 'Marie,

I love you. I will be dead without you. Will you please marry me?'

Her heart had melted. She had looked into the eyes of this man, who had entered her life just a few months ago, and all she had seen was commitment. No one in the world had made her laugh so much, no one had made love to her with such passion and intensity, and no one had ever asked her to marry him.

'Yes,' she had said, partly to see his reaction and partly because that was what she wanted. A small voice inside protested the 'yes', but it was very weak. John had jumped to his feet, picked her up in his arms and done a little dance. Oh, he was so strong and she had felt like a queen that day. Within a few weeks, they were engaged. That had changed things. He became more possessive. He would call her every single day from Kochi and visit every weekend and stay with her in her flat.

But she loved John.

The day after Marie arrived in Mumbai, she visited the office of a famous production company. They had given her an appointment for an audition, but when she got there, she was told that the audition had been postponed. She sat in the reception area for a while, in her carefully selected dress, feeling lonely and angry as the staff behind the desk ignored her. There was a water dispenser in one corner. She drank a glass of water, crushed the plastic glass in anger and walked out after deliberately throwing it on the floor.

Marie decided to visit another production company. She had a list of ten such companies and most of them were located near her hotel. That was the only good thing about it. Fifteen minutes later, she was standing in the reception area of the second production company.

'I'm here for an audition,' she announced, trying to sound confident.

'But there's no audition today.'

She shrugged and kept staring at the women behind the desk. Her beauty didn't work on them.

'You can write your name and other details here and when we have the next audition we will send you an email.' One of the receptionists handed her a register that was so old that its edges had begun to fray.

Marie thought for a moment. She was not someone who was starting out. She had done a few films and several advertisements for popular brands. She returned the register and said, 'No thank you.'

There has to be a better way, she thought as she walked out. By 7 p.m. she had visited three other production companies and received the same response from all of them. She was tired and the rejection was beginning to hurt.

Marie returned to her hotel room and began to cry. A dam somewhere inside her had burst and through it leaked all her confidence.

An hour later, when she saw herself in the mirror, she looked messed up and unattractive. Not even a day old in Mumbai and this cruel city had trampled her looks and self-confidence. She felt like millions of others who had tried to make it in the city and failed.

Her phone began to ring. It was John. Oh, what a relief, she thought as she accepted the call.

'Hi, honey, how are you doing?'

At the sound of his voice, the dam within her broke once again. Marie told him everything between sobs.

'Marie, Bollywood is not a place for good people like you. It's an industry that's full of shit. Every person there is bad.'

'How do you know, John?'

'I always knew it, but when you told me you wanted to go there and try your luck, I didn't want to discourage you. I want you to be happy, Marie. That's what matters to me. Money, fame, success, these things are useless in my dictionary. I'm a soldier and I only know how to live and die for my nation or for those I love.'

His words soothed Marie. She felt better, loved and cared for. All was not lost. She had John. After saying goodbye to him, Marie started to think of a better way to get noticed by the people who mattered. She was good-looking, she was talented and she had experience, so what was it that she did not have?

When she woke up the next morning, the first thing she decided to do was to change her hotel. It was depressing and damp, and it was playing on her nerves. She checked online and selected a well-known four-star hotel. By 1 p.m., she had checked into it. Her room was well-lit, spacious and had a view of the park below.

She ordered a beer and some seafood from room service. As soon as the meal was served, she picked up the mug of beer, dropped the dressing gown she had changed into and slid into the scented bathtub that she had half-filled with soap and water. She sipped her chilled beer. It woke her up. Her confidence was back as she contemplated her next move.

By 3 p.m. she knew what to do. She called all the important people in the Kannada film industry who knew her well—big names, names whose influence was not limited to Bengaluru.

All the people she called were men and they agreed to help.

The first callback came within an hour. 'Marie, write down this address . . .' the man went on to dictate the address.

'Go there at seven today. I hope you are not far and can make it; traffic in Mumbai is crazy.'

'I am close to it and can reach there by seven, earlier if required.'

'Seven is okay. Meet Mr Ganesh Halke. He will be expecting you.'

'Thank you, sir. This means a lot.'

'Oh, come on, Marie, we are friends, aren't we?'

'Yes,' she said before hanging up.

Marie reached the address five minutes before 7 p.m. and asked for Mr Halke. Within minutes, she was escorted to a room in which a camera had been set up. In front of it was a stool. The office boy who had escorted her in asked her to sit on the stool.

After what seemed like ten minutes, bright lights were turned on and a voice said, 'Okay, so show us what you've got. I'm not going to give you any lines. Choose your best lines. You have three minutes.'

Even though she couldn't see anyone because of the lights, she felt comfortable. There were no distractions and the situation worked for her.

Over the next three minutes, Marie acted out her best part. She spoke the lines, stood up, moved about and was happy with her performance when it ended.

'Thank you, but that was not in Hindi. You have to do it in Hindi. Can you come tomorrow? No, wait . . . not tomorrow. Can you come next week?'

'How about right now?'

'Right now? Okay, you've got two minutes. Start.'

Marie's Hindi was weak and she hadn't prepared any lines, but she didn't want to wait a week.

She started tentatively, making lines up, and finished on a high after three minutes. She was happy with her performance, given the circumstances. There were no claps, but who expects claps during auditions?

The lights were turned off and she could now see a man standing behind the camera. He was short, thin and had sunken eyes below an almost-bald head. He appeared to be fifty and had she not seen him in a studio, she would have thought he was a cab driver.

'Thank you. What's your name again?'

'Marie Julia Mohan.'

'Oh, that's a long name. I have recorded your performance; let me speak to my creative team and we will get back to you.'

With that, he was gone. Marie went to the reception and they told her they would call if she was selected.

Over the next three days, Marie auditioned at five different production companies and everyone gave her the same answer. At one of the auditions, she met an executive named Dhiraj. He appeared to be about her age and seemed friendly enough. She asked for his number and he gave it without hesitation. When she didn't hear from anyone over the next few days and realized that the hotel bill was mounting, she decided to call Dhiraj.

'Hi, this is Marie.'

'Marie? Marie . . . wait a minute, we met during your audition a few days back, right?'

'Yes, the same Marie. How are you, Mr Dhiraj?'

'I'm good, thank you. And you?'

'Not so good, actually. I'm still waiting to hear from your company about my audition.'

'Oh, didn't they inform you that you were not selected?'

'No.'

'Well, I'm truly sorry about that, usually we inform . . . but so many people turn up that sometimes it can be difficult. My sincere apologies for making you wait for so long.'

'You don't have to be sorry, Mr Dhiraj.'

'Call me Dhiraj.'

'Dhiraj, I was wondering if we could meet. I'm new to the town and really don't know anyone here.'

'Oh? I was under the impression that you lived in Mumbai.'

'No, I'm from Bangalore.'

'I can't meet you today, but how about tomorrow? At seven?'

'Tomorrow is great.'

'Fabulous, let's meet for a coffee at Zandos. It's a small but interesting café near our office. Suits you?'

'Yes, I look forward to it, Dhiraj. See you.'

'See you.'

As soon as she hung up, she logged into her Facebook account and found Dhiraj's profile. Within minutes, she had learnt whatever she wanted to know. He was twenty-six—the same age as her—and hailed from Kanpur. He appeared to be living alone in Mumbai, where he had moved five years ago and where, like her, he had not known anyone, as he had mentioned in one of his posts.

Marie spent the whole night and the next day thinking about what she would say to Dhiraj. This man was her first and perhaps last hope of getting a toehold in the industry.

The next evening, wearing her favourite dress and looking fresh and pretty, Marie took a taxi to Zandos. On the way, her phone rang. It was John.

'Hi, honey, how are you doing?'

'I'm doing good, just going out to meet someone. Things are looking up.'

'That's so nice to hear. I miss you so much. It has been raining since morning and I wish we were together.'

She heard the longing in her fiancé's voice and felt the same way.

'I wish the same too.'

'Anyway, please take care, don't trust these Mumbaiwalas too much, stick to your work only.'

'I will. Thanks, honey! Bye.'

She hung up and looked outside. It was dusk and suddenly it started to drizzle. It was as if her conversation with her lover had ushered the rain in. She rolled down the window and inhaled the wet air.

It was Marie's turn to call John. 'Honey, guess what? It has started to rain here too. You sent the rain my way.'

'Marie, I swear to God that just after we hung up, I prayed for it to rain in Mumbai too so that you could share the same feeling as me.'

'God listens to you, John.'

'I know. That's why he has given me you, Marie. I love you.'

'I love you too, John.'

When the taxi stopped, Marie paid, held her purse over her head to keep her hair dry and dashed into the café.

Zandos was indeed small with just six tables. There was a counter on one side and one wall was made entirely of glass so that people could look outside. Marie took a table for two. Only one other table was occupied.

A girl in an apron appeared by her side. Marie looked up and asked, 'Can I use the washroom?'

The girl pointed to one corner and Marie walked into a tiny bathroom with a small mirror. She spent the next five minutes adjusting her hair and touching-up, emerging only when she felt confident. When she sat down at the table again, she looked at her watch. It was five minutes to seven.

Dhiraj arrived at seven on the dot. He gave her a big smile as he walked across to where she sat. He was wearing a black half-sleeved shirt, unbuttoned, the tight white tee that he wore underneath visible. Faded blue jeans and black sneakers completed the look. He was slim, handsome and had a charming smile that put Marie at ease immediately.

'Hi, Marie, it's lovely to see you again.'

'Same here, Dhiraj. Thank you for taking the time out to meet someone like me.'

'Oh, come on. So you are new to Mumbai, is it?'

'Yes.'

'I was once new too, this place can be cruel . . .'

The waitress appeared by their side and he paused to ask, 'So, what will you have, Marie?'

After both of them ordered coffees, they continued chatting. Dhiraj was a simple but ambitious person who appeared to have done all the right things to get where he was. He told her about his dream of making Bollywood films one day.

'So, do you have a boyfriend?'

The question caught Marie off guard. It occurred to her that if she told him the truth, he would lose interest and perhaps her only chance to get somewhere in Bollywood would wither away.

'No, of course not.'

'And I don't have a girlfriend. So, tell me, what are you doing tonight?'

'I'm here with you.'

'This is evening. It's just eight. In Mumbai, the night starts at ten.'

'Well, nothing, I was planning to go back to my hotel and rest.' She deliberately mentioned the name of the hotel and saw him take note of it. Under no circumstance did she want him to know how desperate her situation was.

'Great! Then let me pick you up around ten thirty from your hotel. Let's dine together.'

Marie was excited but played it cool. She could sense the effect she was having on Dhiraj and knew exactly what he wanted. The situation could not have been better for her.

'Sure, it will be a pleasure.'

Marie took a taxi back to her hotel. She didn't have a problem sleeping with Dhiraj if it came to that, but that would mean cheating on John. Marie had maintained relations with many men, but she had ended them after her engagement. In the end, she decided to keep the evening short and flirty.

Dhiraj arrived at the hotel five minutes early. He planted a polite kiss on her cheek and she did the same. Soon, she was seated in the back seat of a luxury sedan. Dhiraj was clearly out to impress her. He was dressed in a silk shirt, matching trousers and shoes that shone even in the dark. Marie was wearing a short skirt, which rode high as she sat.

The car soon pulled into the driveway of a five-star hotel. Marie didn't know if Dhiraj owned the car. If he did, which was the impression she got based on his instructions to the driver and his body language, he was doing well for himself in the film industry. He extended his hand and she took it. They walked into the hotel hand in hand, like two people who knew each other well; they could have been best friends, or even lovers.

After they were seated in the restaurant, Dhiraj asked, 'So, what would you like to drink?'

'Thanks, Dhiraj, but I'll have a drink on the condition that we split the bill.'

'You are my date, Marie, so don't worry about the bill. Now, your drink of preference, please.'

She settled for vodka while Dhiraj ordered a whisky. After two rounds, they were talking like old friends. Dhiraj got up and sat next to her on the upholstered double seat. He casually put his arm around her. Marie knew where things were headed, but his conversation was music to her ears. Dhiraj had told her that most auditions were a sham, but that he would help her get roles. He had influence not just in his company but also in the industry.

He pulled her close and she turned to look at him. Their eyes met and he leant in. Marie closed her eyes as she felt his lips on hers. They were trembling. Part of her was excited to be desired by such a handsome young man, but part of her resisted. He moved his lips against hers and soon the kiss became more passionate. She found herself giving in to the sensation. It felt good.

They heard someone clearing his throat. It was the steward asking if they needed anything else. Using the opportunity, Marie got up and sat on the chair Dhiraj had earlier occupied. Dhiraj, meanwhile, ordered more drinks.

'Arre, what happened?'

'This is a public place.' It was the best excuse she could give under the circumstances. She wanted to stop what was going on, but at the same time she didn't want to annoy Dhiraj.

'I agree.'

After that it was all business. Dhiraj asked her to come to his office at 10 a.m. the following day and promised that he would have something worthwhile for her in just a few days. Marie was ecstatic. Her career in Bollywood seemed like an achievable possibility.

When the car pulled into the porch of Marie's hotel, she got out. Then she bent down to thank Dhiraj through the window. He smiled, his expression uncertain. Marie knew all she had to do was ask and he would accompany her to her room. But she turned on her heel and walked into the hotel, alone.

She had barely reached her room when her phone rang. It was Dhiraj.

'Yes, Dhiraj?'

'I forgot to tell you something, Marie. You are the most beautiful woman I have ever met. I enjoyed your company and can hardly wait for tomorrow.'

'Same here, Dhiraj. Thank you.'

'I like you, Marie. I like you a lot.'

She knew alcohol was partly responsible for his words, but she also knew that he spoke the truth. He seemed to be smitten with her. Marie changed and went to bed, her head filled with possibilities of what the next few days could bring. When she finally fell asleep, she was smiling.

The next day, after speaking to John but omitting any mention of her evening, she left for Dhiraj's office, getting there at 10 a.m. on the dot. He was already there and his interaction with her was businesslike even though he smiled broadly when he saw her. They were seated in Dhiraj's office. She was impressed that he had a cabin to himself.

'Marie, based on the audition you gave a few days ago, our company would like to sign you for a role in our upcoming project. It's a big-budget film and you will play the part of the hero's first girlfriend who dies in an accident. It's a ten-minute role. But there's a song and you will be featured opposite a top star.'

She got up and hugged him. The contract was signed by the afternoon. The money she was being paid would see her through the next few months.

That evening, Dhiraj dropped her off at her hotel. This time she invited him to her room. It was 8 p.m. and they ordered a few drinks from room service. By 10 p.m., Dhiraj was all over her and, this time, Marie didn't stop him. She gave in wholeheartedly to the man who had won her heart. The sex was mind-blowing. Dhiraj was gentle when she needed and rough when he wanted something. He stayed over that night. They made love three more times during the night and once in the morning, just after breakfast.

As Dhiraj was leaving, she told him that she had some errands to take care of and would reach his office by the afternoon.

Marie knew she had committed a sin. She went to a church she had seen in the neighbourhood and prayed. She asked for forgiveness. Later, on her way to his office, she decided to end things with Dhiraj. She already had the role, the money would be paid soon and in the meantime she could look for a decent flat.

But things did not go the way she had planned. Just the sight of Dhiraj weakened her resolve. On the way back to her hotel that evening, Dhiraj said, 'Marie, you can now rent a flat. It's more economical and practical.'

'Yes, I was thinking the same thing.'

'I can help you get a great place. Look, why don't you shift to my place until we find a flat for you?'

'No, no. That's not right.'

'Don't worry, I won't bother you.' He winked.

Without wanting to, she found herself agreeing to his proposal and checked out of the hotel that same evening. Dhiraj lived in a small one-bedroom flat. But the society it was located in was posh and the location excellent. The next few days were like a honeymoon for her. Dhiraj wanted her more and more and she found herself giving in more and more.

Finally, after three days, Dhiraj told her, 'I have found the perfect flat for you. It's just a kilometre from here. It's nice and well within your budget.'

Marie was relieved. Staying away from Dhiraj would help her focus on John again. She completed the paperwork the next day and decided to shift to her new flat the same evening.

Dhiraj drove her to the flat. She opened the door. There was a sofa in the living room, a ceiling fan, a small side table and an air conditioner. The kitchen had a hob and basic utensils and crockery. The only bedroom had two mattresses on the floor. There was an air conditioner and a ceiling fan too. Thankfully, Marie noticed, all the windows had curtains. She inspected the bathroom and found it to be clean, with running water.

'Do you like it?'

'This is lovely.' She had signed the lease on Dhiraj's assurance and she was not disappointed. For Rs 40,000 a month, the flat was a steal.

'Marie, I'll help you settle in here.'

'There is nothing to settle in. I think you should go home now. I will invite you over when I convert this into a proper house, my house.'

But once again things didn't go the way she had planned.

After placing her suitcase in the bedroom, he reclined on the mattress and announced, 'How can I leave my sweetheart alone? I will stay with you for a couple of days, help you buy stuff and settle in before I move out.'

Marie placed her hands on her hips and looked at him. His expression was sincere. He wanted to help and she realized that she didn't mind. Except that it was becoming difficult to hide the fact that she was engaged to someone else. And that she was in love with the man she was engaged to. Over the past few days, she had been comparing the two men and realized that her heart still belonged to John. He was her man. Dhiraj was an extra who was good and generous and obviously liked her a lot, but she didn't love him.

She decided to try again. 'Dhiraj, you must go now. Please.'

Dhiraj got up and pulled her into an embrace. Once again, she forgot her resolve as soon as he kissed her. After they had finished and Dhiraj had gone to the bathroom, Marie's phone rang. It was John. So far, she had not told him anything about Dhiraj. John was so possessive that she was sure he would create a ruckus. All she had told him was that she had moved in to a friend's house.

'Hi, sweetheart, how are you doing?'

'Great, just shifted, honey.'

'I wish I was there to help, Marie.'

'It's no big deal. I just have one suitcase and a few other basic items.'

She heard Dhiraj opening the bathroom door and walking towards her.

'Marie, where is the towel?' Dhiraj said before Marie could cover the mouthpiece with her hand.

'Who's that in your house, Marie?'

'Nobody. Just a friend who's helping me move.' She gestured to Dhiraj to remain quiet.

'A man?'

'Yes, he helped me get this role. Just a friend.'

'Marie, tell him to leave. I don't want him to stay in your house for the night.'

'Of course, why would he stay here? He was just leaving.'

When John hung up, Marie knew that he hadn't liked what he had heard. She turned to Dhiraj, who was looking at her. 'Why did you have to speak so loudly?'

'Who was that?'

'My fiancé.'

'Fiancé? So, who am I? You said you didn't have anyone in your life, didn't you?'

'Dhiraj, look, I like you. I made the mistake of hiding the fact that I'm engaged. But I felt so helpless that my heart wouldn't listen to me.'

'Honey, I love you. I really do. I was going to propose soon.'

She moved away from him. 'Look, we shouldn't discuss this today. We can talk some other time. Please, go home now.'

'I won't go, Marie, I told you so. I want to stay here with you.'

'Suit yourself.'

Dhiraj got them takeaway from a nearby restaurant and they slept soon after eating.

The next morning, Marie woke up to the shrill sound of the doorbell. It was 7 a.m. She yawned and walked across the living room to open the door.

The sight of the person at her door shocked her. It was John. He pushed her aside and entered the house. He went straight to the bedroom and saw Dhiraj sleeping on the mattress. He turned and shouted at Marie, 'You fucking bitch, what did I tell you?'

Dhiraj woke up and looked at the two of them, dazed. John slapped Marie. Dhiraj struggled to get up and took two steps towards them, warning John not to touch Marie. At this, John turned towards Dhiraj and punched him. Dhiraj went reeling back, his head hitting the wall. John looked around. He was wild with rage. From where he stood, he could see the entrance to the kitchen. He dashed into it and emerged a few seconds later with a knife. Even before Dhiraj could comprehend the danger he was in, John stabbed him in the stomach. He continued to stab him until Dhiraj crashed to the floor.

Dhiraj died within a few minutes as John stood watching him, breathing heavily. Marie kept staring at the knife in his hands. After a few minutes, John checked Dhiraj's pulse and turned to look at Marie. 'He is dead because of you.'

Marie didn't say anything as John grabbed her by the waist. He first undressed her and then himself. Then he pushed her down on to the mattress that was next to the one on which Dhiraj lay dead. John entered her with great force and the two of them made love.

Later, he said, 'Marie, we need to get rid of this man.'

She nodded. John instructed her to purchase several items and Marie left to buy them from a nearby mall. After she was back with several large plastic bags, ropes and a knife, John dragged the body into the kitchen and began to cut it into pieces so that they could put them into the bags. It took him almost four hours to stuff the body parts into three large plastic bags. Marie helped him with whatever he told her to do.

Halfway through the hacking, he asked her to arrange for a car. Marie had made a few other acquaintances in Dhiraj's production company and she called one of them. She told the man that she needed a car as she had to go to Dadar to shop. He agreed to loan her his Santro for a day and drove it to her apartment. John and Marie took the bags down in the lift and placed them in the boot of the borrowed car even as the guard looked on.

'Where are we going?' asked Marie.

'Far, but we will be back by the evening.'

On the way, Dhiraj's mobile, which Marie had kept in her purse, started to ring. She pulled it out to check who was calling but accidently pressed the 'accept' button. As soon as she realized her mistake, she pressed the 'end' button.

On the outskirts of Mumbai, they stopped to buy two bottles of petrol. Finally, they reached a village near a place called Naigaon by 5 p.m. Selecting a secluded spot, they poured petrol over the body parts and burnt them. After this they drove back to Mumbai, reaching the city by 9 p.m. On the way back, Dhiraj's phone rang again. This time, Marie answered it deliberately. She told the caller that Dhiraj had left her flat at midnight but had forgotten his phone. Then, she switched his phone off.

Back home, the two of them changed and went to a local eatery for dinner.

The following day, John went into hiding, but he called Marie regularly to check on the progress of the investigation. Both knew that Dhiraj's father had filed a missing person's report. On the third day, accompanied by Dhiraj's friends and relatives, Marie went to the police station and demanded to know why the investigation was proceeding so slowly.

The police formed a team. They checked Dhiraj's call log and were able to determine the location of his phone on the night that he had disappeared, based on the two calls that were made to his number. Both had been received on the outskirts of Mumbai. One of the callers told the police that a woman had answered the phone and said that Dhiraj had been with her earlier, but had forgotten his phone at her house. Since the police knew Dhiraj was last seen with Marie they started to question her. Their doubts were confirmed when Marie told them that she had been shopping in Dadar that evening. How could she have been in Dadar and on the outskirts of Mumbai at the same time?

The police suspected that Marie was involved in the case in some way or she wouldn't have lied. They called her to the police station, confident that they would be able to learn the truth.

'How did you go to Dadar?' Inspector Lokhande, the investigating officer, asked her.

'I borrowed a naval officer's car.'

'Name please?'

She gave them the name of John's friend. He had told her to give this name if the police asked.

One of the members of the investigating team got in touch with the naval authorities and spoke to the officer. He told the police that he hadn't loaned his car to anyone and had, in fact, been out at sea that day.

'The officer said he did not loan you his car,' Inspector Lokhande informed her.

The investigating team had also learnt that during the past few weeks someone called John Varghese had called Marie's number more than a thousand times.

'Who is John Varghese?'

'He's my fiancé. What has he got to do with this?'

Marie felt the noose tightening around her neck. She went back home, called John and told him everything.

The next day, the police continued with the investigation. 'Ms Marie, whose car did you take to Dadar that day?'

'I took my friend's Santro.' She gave them the right name this time. She knew there was nothing to worry about as John had got the car washed properly before returning it.

The police searched the car and found traces of blood. When tested in a laboratory, the samples matched Dhiraj's blood. This meant that the body had been carried in the Santro. When the police interrogated the watchman of the building where Marie lived, they learnt about the black bags that John and Marie had carried out of the building. They now had enough information to corner Marie. When she realized that the police had put together all the pieces of the jigsaw, Marie told them the truth and was taken into custody.

John was arrested the next day from Kochi.

Over the next few months, the police built a watertight case, which led to both Marie and John being convicted. While Marie got three years in jail, John got ten years.

Interesting fact: Once she was out of jail, Marie was accused of duping several businessmen of over Rs 30 crore. Her method was simple. Along with another woman whom she had befriended in jail, she scouted for businessmen in need of money. Convincing them of their connections with banks, the two women would ask for a 10 per cent advance as commission. After the commission was paid, they would end all communication with the loan aspirants. The cheated men could not trace them as the names given to them were fake and the phone numbers temporary. Piecing together all the information from several complaints, the police drew up a list of suspects. Marie's name was on that list, but when they got to the address where she had supposedly been living since her release, they found that the house had been vacated. As of January 2019, all of Mumbai Police's efforts to trace Marie failed and no one has any idea where she is.

6

The Triple Murder

When Sneha first saw her future lover, she was eating ice cream. It was June and the only way to beat the heat outside the beauty parlour where she worked was to eat something cold. And since she was a child, ice cream had been her preference.

Like Sneha, the man who was staring at her was young, around twenty-three years old. He was tall, and under the tight T-shirt and jeans that he was wearing, he appeared to be strong and athletic. His unruly hair fell over his broad forehead. His smile was his best feature, making his eyes sparkle. He seemed friendly. Sneha could tell by his body language that he was interested in her.

At first, she decided to ignore him. Sneha was attractive and almost every other man, young or old, was interested in her. God had given her a beautiful face, but Sneha also had a knack for dressing well. She also watched her diet to ensure she remained slim. Ice cream was her only occasional indulgence.

She walked away from the ice cream stall, the half-eaten cone still in her hand. From the shopping complex, which was in Indore's Sanjay Nagar area, she walked towards the municipality park.

The park's entrance was about 100 metres away. Halfway there, she turned to look back. The man was about 20 metres behind her. She paused for a fraction of a second, hoping that the man would raise his hand to say hello. But he didn't, so she tossed her head, her shoulder-length hair swaying around her oval face, and resumed walking.

By the time she reached the gate, she had finished her ice cream. She threw the wrapper into a bin near the entrance and stepped into the park. Instead of taking the walking track that ran along the periphery of the park, she walked across the soft grass towards a bench.

She sat down on the bench and turned to look towards the gate. The man had stopped there, probably wondering what to do next.

Sneha smiled at him. It wasn't a broad smile, just a tiny gesture, an opening for the man to take. The man remained expressionless and kept staring at her. He was probably a pervert with only one thing on his mind—to ravage her— Sneha thought. But she was not the kind to be scared of people like him. In her purse, she carried a knife, which she had used twice in the past for self-defence, succeeding both times in scaring her attacker away. She was also strong enough to put up a good fight.

Sneha had only one ambition—she wanted to get rich, quickly. She was prepared to go to any lengths.

Sneha had everything going for her, except an education. She had studied only till class X. She could have studied more had her family's circumstances not put her under pressure to earn money. But she knew that there were many uneducated people who had managed to get rich. She wanted to be one of them.

The man finally decided to approach her. Sneha watched him out of the corner of her eye. His gait was sure, his eyes were on her, and when he stopped near her, she could hear his breathing. Without looking up, Sneha opened her purse and placed her hand around the handle of the knife, out of his sight. Then she looked up.

'Kya dekhta hai bey? Kabhi ladki nahi dekhi kya [What are you looking at? Have you never seen a girl before]?'

'Itni sundar nahi dekhi [No one as beautiful as you].'

With that, before she could do anything, he bent down, pulled her off the bench and kissed her. Sneha felt powerless for the first time in her life. Her grip on the handle of the knife gave way and she found herself kissing him back.

The man suddenly shouted in pain and stepped away from her. Sneha fell back on to the bench, her reflexes saving her from falling.

A policeman had hit the man on his buttocks.

'Abbe yeh kya kar rahe ho salon, ye park hai, tumhara randikhana nahin [What are you two up to? This is a park, not a brothel].'

Sneha looked at the man who had kissed her. His eyes were like embers. The policeman flinched as he stared at him.

The policeman raised his baton again, but this time when he brought it down, the man caught it halfway.

'Bas. Nahi to . . . [Stop, or . . .]'

The policeman was clearly scared. But he did not give up easily. 'Nahi to? Saale, nahi to kya karega tu [Or? What will you do]?'

Instead of answering, the man turned around and walked away. The policeman turned to the woman. 'Kya lagta hai wo tera [How do you know him]?'

'Mera premi hai, sahib. Hum dono ek dusre se bahut pyaar karte hain [He is my lover. We love each other a lot].'

She laughed at her silly reply, feeling guilty but also excited. The policeman too turned and walked away.

A few people had gathered around and were now staring at Sneha. She looked at them and said, 'Mujhse shaadi karega woh. Lekin mujhe nahi pata main haan kahungi ya na [He wants to marry me, but I don't know if I will say yes or not].'

The story she had fabricated made her laugh again. She had the power in this situation. The man wanted her, but the real question was: did she want him?

She knew the answer deep down in her heart. There was something in the man's eyes. She knew he was the kind of man she wanted—someone who not only found her attractive but also was not scared of anyone, not even the police.

Sneha had met him on a Sunday. So, the following Sunday, having taken extra care to look her best, she approached the same ice cream vendor near the shopping complex. She bought an ice cream, unwrapped it, licked it and turned around to look at the same spot where she had seen him for the first time.

He was there. The same eyes, the same quiet stance. This couldn't be happening, she thought.

Sneha waved at him. He walked towards the ice cream stall, his eyes on her. Sneha felt self-conscious and dropped her eyes, but she raised them when he came and stood next to her.

'My name is Rakesh. I love you.'

She laughed. He had not even asked what her name was or what she did or what she thought about that day when he had kissed her without her consent. But there was one good thing in this. He didn't care who she was, what she did, whether she had money or not, what her religion or caste was, nothing. He was interested only in who she was as a person.

'My name is Sneha.'

'Can we talk?'

'Yes, let's go to the park,' she said but then remembered the policeman.

'No, wait. Let's go to the coffee shop over there.' She pointed towards a café not far from where they stood.

Sneha discarded the ice cream in a dustbin and walked with him towards the café. She had never let go of or even shared her ice cream with anyone before. She was so excited that she didn't even realize what she had done.

Over the next two hours, they learnt everything about each other. Like Sneha, all Rakesh wanted was to make money and become rich. He had already been in jail twice due to his carelessness, but he was confident that he would make no mistake the next time.

Sneha was over the moon. That evening, the two of them checked into a cheap lodge and made love. Sneha, who had slept with a few men in the past, found Rakesh to be different. They ate together in the room, drank whisky and made more love.

After that night, they met almost every evening. Soon, Rakesh and Sneha realized that they were meant to be with each other for the rest of their lives. But to live happily as man and wife, they needed money, something that they constantly talked about.

About a month later, Sneha had a fight with the owner of the parlour where she worked and was fired. She called Rakesh, who was working as a welder not far away.

'Rakesh, meri naukri gayi yaar. Jaldi aa [I have lost my job, please come fast].'

That day, as she ran into his arms, Sneha cried. She had been fired because she had stolen a few items from the parlour and had been caught on camera.

'Lekin meri kya galti hai bata? Mujhe woh items chahiye the bas [What is my fault? I just wanted those things].'

Rakesh nodded. He told her that he understood and that she was not at fault.

'Aise nahin chalega, darling. Kuch to karna padega [It won't work this way. We have to do something about this].'

Rakesh nodded again; several ideas were floating around in his mind. But he knew that this time he would have to be very careful. He didn't want his carelessness to cost Sneha.

Over the next two months, they tried to come up with a workable plan. In the meantime, Sneha joined a company that sold cosmetics door-to-door.

One evening, while she was at a mall trying to woo customers, Sneha came across a middle-aged woman who was wearing a lot of gold jewellery.

'Madam, if you sign up to become a member of our company, you can get branded cosmetics at a very cheap rate.'

The woman walked away, saying, 'No, I'm not interested.'

'Please give me at least two minutes to tell you about the offer. I'm sure you won't be able to say "no".'

'Okay.'

Sneha started with her sales pitch but ended up making a mess of it. Finally, when she stopped, the woman said, 'I'm still not sure what I will gain out of this.'

'Can I have an appointment to meet you some other time?'

Sneha was fascinated by the woman and wasn't prepared to let her go easily. She had done a quick calculation of the worth of all the gold jewellery the woman was wearing. It must be worth over Rs 20 lakh. How much would this woman have in her home!

'Well, I'm not sure I want to be part of this . . .' the woman finally said.

'Can I have your number? Please ma'am, please.'

She shrugged and gave Sneha her number before walking away.

The woman's name was Meera Deshmukh and she lived in Sanjay Nagar, not far from the mall. She lived with her seventy-year-old mother, Nandini, and her twenty-one-year-old daughter, Asha. Her husband worked as a factory manager and they had moved to Indore from Jabalpur just a week before.

Sneha quietly followed the woman and saw her getting into a big, chauffeur-driven car. Without a doubt, the woman was loaded. A plan began to form in Sneha's mind. She left the mall and called Rakesh.

'Rakesh, jaan, aa ja, plan banate hain. Ek murgi hai. Moti wali [Come soon. Let's plan. I have a target in mind].'

Rakesh was excited when they met at the lodge. First they made love and then Sneha told him all about the woman she had just met.

'Lekin isme plan kya hai [But what's the plan]?'

'Bas wohi to banana hai. Tere paas bandook hain na [We have to work that out. You have a pistol, right]?'

Rakesh nodded.

Sneha convinced Rakesh that they would easily get anything between Rs 50 lakh to Rs 1 crore from the woman. She expected that much money and jewellery to be in her house.

Rakesh said they needed another man, someone they could trust and who was experienced. Sneha agreed and Rakesh called his friend Mohit, who instantly agreed to be a part of their plan.

But first they needed an opportunity to enter the house without being stopped. Sneha called Meera Deshmukh.

'Ma'am, good evening. This is Sneha. I met you at the mall yesterday.'

'Yes, tell me.'

'Ma'am, please give me one more chance to explain how my company's membership plan can help you. I need just ten minutes. Yesterday, you gave me only two minutes and I could not explain things properly.'

Sneha had used her sweetest voice and her heart was beating fast. A lot depended on this call.

'Sure, can you come to my house at four tomorrow?'

'Thank you very much, ma'am. Please tell me your address.'

Meera gave her the address. As Sneha hung up, she was smiling from ear to ear. Soon, the plan was finalized. Sneha would drive her scooty to the building where Meera lived while the men would get there on a stolen motorcycle. They would meet outside the building and proceed together. Sneha would ring the doorbell while the other two would remain out of sight. Rakesh would carry the pistol and Sneha and Mohit would hide a knife under their clothes. The plan was to scare Meera with the pistol, ask for the keys and make good with the loot. No killings, it was decided.

The next day, the three met near the staircase of the apartment building where the Deshmukhs lived. It was time for action. They went up to Meera's flat and Sneha rang the doorbell. She was excited—in less than fifteen minutes, she and Rakesh would be very rich. She was not scared one bit. As she waited, she turned to look at Rakesh and Mohit, who were standing out of the range of the peephole. They seemed to be ready.

The door was opened by an old woman Sneha had never seen before. She was surprised but maintained her cool. 'I'm here to meet Meera ma'am.'

The old woman sized her up from top to bottom, turned around and, leaving the door open, shouted, 'Meera!'

Sneha took two steps inside as the old woman's head was turned away and signalled to the men. They came inside too and Sneha closed the door.

The old woman turned back and found herself facing three people instead of one.

'Who are you?'

Rakesh stepped forward and pulled out his country-made pistol from his pocket. 'If you make any noise, we will kill you.'

The old woman was not prepared for this. She opened her mouth to scream and Rakesh raised his pistol and fired. The bullet entered the side of her head. The woman slumped to the floor noiselessly.

Since no one came out to see what the commotion was about, the three moved further into the house. They pushed open one of the doors, which led to a bedroom, and saw Meera and another young woman watching television.

Rakesh raised his pistol again. 'If you make a sound, I will kill you.'

Next, Sneha demanded the keys to the safe. Meera had recognized Sneha; she got up and gave her the keys without a word. Sneha handed the keys to Mohit who opened the safe in the already-open cupboard.

There was a lot of cash inside and also several boxes of jewellery. He pulled them all out. Sneha looked at Rakesh and exchanged smiles.

Meera said softly, 'Please take everything and go.'

'Will you inform the police?' Sneha asked.

'No.'

Rakesh turned towards Sneha. 'Are you out of your mind? We have killed one woman. We can't leave these two or they will tell the police.'

'Oh my God, my mother!' Meera looked towards the door and got up. She had forgotten about her mother, and because of the noise from the television, she had not heard the gunshot.

In a flash, Rakesh aimed at Meera but the gun fired a second late as it was country-made and prone to a faulty trigger mechanism. By then, his hand had come down and the bullet hit him in the leg. He shouted in pain as Sneha grabbed Meera. Being stronger than Meera, she successfully pushed her back on to the bed.

Rakesh was now crying in pain. Mohit looked on from near the cupboard while Sneha stood next to the bed. Things were not going according to plan and the three were not sure what to do next. Taking advantage of this, Meera began to shout for help.

Sneha pulled out her knife and took a wild swipe at Meera. The blade sliced Meera's throat and she fell down, clutching her bleeding neck.

Mohit ran towards Asha, who had been too scared to react or speak. But seeing Mohit charge towards her, holding a knife, she began to shout too. Mohit stabbed her in the chest. Both Sneha and Mohit kept stabbing their victims for the next few minutes. When they were sure the women were dead, they finally stopped and looked at Rakesh. By now Sneha and Mohit were completely covered in blood.

Sneha told Mohit, 'Bring the old woman's body into this room.'

Once that was done, Rakesh whispered, his voice breaking due to the pain from the bullet wound, 'Sneha, we have to get away quickly.'

'Yes, my love,' she said and started to put all the jewellery and money that was scattered on the floor into a large bag that she had found in the cupboard. When she was done, she quickly rummaged through the cupboard and found two ATM cards. She pocketed them as well.

They washed up in the adjoining bathroom and left the house right after. Fortunately, no one saw them leaving the building. It was a successful operation except for the fact that Rakesh had been shot.

There was a small dispensary run by an Ayurvedic doctor close to where Sneha lived. She sent Mohit away and took Rakesh there.

The doctor was shocked but said nothing.

Sneha explained, 'Goli lagi hai. Gunde aaye the hamare gaon mein. Jaldi kuch karo [It's a bullet wound. Dacoits attacked our village. We need help].'

The doctor cleaned the wound and said after a few minutes, 'Goli bahut andar hai, hospital hi jana padega. Nahi toh . . . [The bullet is lodged deep inside. You must take him to a hospital, or . . .]'

'Nahi toh [Or]?'

'I'm sorry, jaldi karna hoga [You must hurry].'

Sneha looked at Rakesh who nodded. Half an hour later, Rakesh was admitted to a private hospital. Sneha stuck to the story that they didn't know who had fired at them. The men who had attacked them were dacoits, she explained.

Meanwhile, a neighbour noticed bloody footprints leading away from the Deshmukhs' door. She immediately called the police. The police arrived within minutes as the thana was just a kilometre away.

The house was latched from the outside—Sneha and her gang had done this on their way out. The police opened the door. What they saw chilled them to their bones. Even the police had not seen such a gruesome sight in an urban space before.

They started their investigation methodically. Jorawar Singh Yadav led the team. They cordoned off the area, took pictures of the crime scene, sent samples for forensic investigation, collected evidence and spoke to the neighbours. Since the safe was open, with all the valuables stolen, the motive was clear. But one puzzle remained. While they found two empty shells, they could not find the second bullet. The first was in the body of the one of the victims, but there was no trace of the second bullet.

Since nobody had seen the killers come and go, and there were no security cameras, it was like searching for a needle in a haystack. Their only hope was solving the mystery of the second bullet.

The forensic team had got fingerprints from the latch of the main door and from the safe in the bedroom. They had also collected blood samples from the bathroom. The blood, they knew from experience, didn't belong to the victims. Collecting samples from the bathroom was a painstaking and difficult exercise as it involved dismantling the drains in the bathroom to extract samples from the accumulated human debris.

Jorawar's team struck gold when the blood and the fingerprints matched those of someone in their records. The man's name was Rakesh Singh, but when they got to his address they couldn't find him. The police team launched a search for Rakesh in the city. Roadblocks were set up on the outskirts in case the suspect tried to escape. The bus station, railway station and airport were also put under surveillance. But for the next twenty-four hours, the police did not get any leads.

The murder had taken the city by storm. The police were under tremendous pressure from the media. The home minister of the state called the director general of police in Bhopal, who gave a televised statement saying that every effort was being made to arrest the killers.

What was bothering Jorawar more than anything else, however, was the mystery of the missing bullet. He discussed many theories with his team, but nothing seemed to make sense. Then, while sipping tea and pondering over the case, a thought crossed his mind. He smiled and called his deputy. 'Contact all the hospitals in the city and find out if anyone was admitted with a bullet wound in the last two days.'

The police's efforts yielded results in just one hour.

Jorawar was at the hospital with his team within fifteen minutes. There, he met the victim of the gunshot wound and his girlfriend. Both were in their twenties and claimed that he had been shot at by dacoits.

However, his deputy had a picture of the man whose fingerprints and blood had been found at the crime site. When he compared the picture with the man on the hospital bed, there was no doubt about the similarity.

But Sneha was clean. She was beautiful and innocent-looking. No one imagined that she was in fact the mastermind behind the robbery and triple murder. However, under the pressure of police questioning, she admitted to the crime. Mohit too was arrested the same evening.

The police thus managed to solve the case in less than three days. After the investigations were complete, the sessions court announced the death penalty for all three, saying that they did not deserve mercy. Further, the court added, the case was a rare one as three helpless women, belonging to three different generations, had been murdered for quick money.

Interesting fact: Sneha was presented with a national award two years after being convicted, while she was in jail waiting to be hanged. She learnt how to do zardozi work while in jail and taught the skill to other woman inmates. She also shared her knowledge about beauty treatments and personal hygiene with other inmates. Sneha was one of eight women inmates in India who were recognized and awarded.

7

The Honeytrap

Fifty-one-year-old Madhu Goyal sat in a café in Islamabad's Jinnah market. The temperature outside was 5° Celsius on that winter day in 2009. But inside, she was comfortable thanks to the heating. As always, she had taken care with her clothes and appearance. Though she was slightly plump, her large eyes, long hair and well-groomed personality never failed to impress and attract people.

She had arrived a few minutes earlier in her car, which was parked in its usual spot, an indication that the meeting was on. The man she was waiting to meet liked her a lot. Not only did he find her beautiful—he had professed his admiration for her numerous times during the past six months of knowing her—but he also loved everything about her: her proficiency in Urdu, her interest in Sufi music and her belief that India and Pakistan were just one nation divided by an arbitrary line.

'Mashallah! You look gorgeous today.'

The man, Jamaal, or Jammy as she preferred to call him, walked up to her. Madhu's heart skipped a beat. In fact, it skipped two beats that evening. One, because he looked so handsome in his Pathani suit, a mix of casual, traditional and earthy and, two, because the word 'gorgeous' had sent a wave of excitement through her body.

She adjusted the elaborately embroidered dupatta over her blue kameez, the mirror work on which reflected the bright lights of the café, and said, 'Thank you, Jammy. Ghazab toh aap bhi lag rahe ho [You look great yourself].'

He slid into the seat opposite hers and looked at her through eyes that twinkled with happiness as he took her hands into his own. Madhu shivered. She wanted him to hold her in his arms right then. But that would have to wait; as always, they needed to be discreet.

'Have you got what I wanted?'

'Of course.'

She pulled out an envelope from her purse and passed it to him. He grabbed it, looked around casually and opened it. While he read through the few papers that were in the envelope, Madhu thought about the situation. Every few days, Jamaal would ask her to get him some information from the Indian High Commission where she worked as a second press secretary. He had told her that he traded it for the money they would need for their future together.

Madhu didn't mind sharing the documents as, according to her, they were not secret in nature. She was also not worried that these nuggets of information might fall into the wrong hands. Madhu was certain that she wasn't sharing anything that could create trouble for the India–Pakistan relationship. Above all, she trusted Jammy. He had assured her that he would protect the identity of his informer with his own life.

'Our love is above this,' he had said the first time she had asked him to be careful. They were together in bed at that time, his hands all over her.

'Arre, where are you lost, my love?'

Jamaal's sudden question brought her back to the café they were sitting in.

'Oh, nothing, I was just thinking about . . .'

'Us. You were thinking about us, right?'

'Yes,' she felt herself blush. The look in his eyes made it clear what was on his mind. He wanted her right at that moment. Jammy, the man Madhu was so in love with, wanted to make love to her.

It was the perfect time for the two of them to leave and carry the evening forward.

They left separately, just as they had come, but headed to the same destination, arriving separately as well. Once united in their regular room at the nondescript safe house, which was about five kilometres from Jinnah market, they wasted no time in reclaiming each other's bodies.

Half an hour later, he asked her, 'Madhu, tea?'

'Yes, I'm dying for it.'

Jammy prepared tea in a pot. Their choice in tea was similar. In fact, their preference for traditional clothes, their love for Urdu poetry and their outlook on life were just some of the many similarities they shared.

Sipping her tea, Madhu whispered, 'It's so quiet here, Jammy.'

'I think time has slowed down too.'

She smiled as they sat drinking tea, he naked except for his briefs and she only partly dressed.

'Madhu, I want you to promise me that you will not meet any Pakistani man except me.'

This was unexpected, an aberration in Jammy's otherwise gentlemanly behaviour. From time to time, he would come up with such odd demands.

'What?' she looked up sharply, 'Why would you say that, Jammy?'

'I repeat. I don't want you to meet any other Pakistani man. This is important. I don't want any discussion on this.'

'Jamaal, what are you saying? My job requires me to meet many people, many of them men, but it is purely business. I have no other intentions. You know that, don't you? Please understand.'

'There is nothing to understand, Madhu. I don't want you to meet any other Pakistani man, that's all.'

'But why are you so possessive?'

He pulled her close and kissed her passionately. 'Did you get your answer?'

His possessiveness initially gave Madhu a high. But after a few seconds, her thoughts turned towards trust. Why would a man she loved so dearly and took so much risk for not trust her?

Madhu decided to change the topic and steered the conversation towards their marriage, which they talked about often. Within minutes, the discussion led to another confrontation. This was clearly not a good day for the two of them, thought a frustrated Madhu.

'As my wife, you will have to follow the rules of our house,' said Jammy.

'I'm ready to follow all the rules, make all the sacrifices that are necessary, but I can't be a typical housewife in purdah.'

He didn't say anything but looked away as Madhu continued, 'I'm an educated woman, Jammy. Partying with men, *sher-o-shayari*, dancing and drinking wine sometimes, all these are a part of my personality, my world.'

He turned to look at her. 'I know, but here in Pakistan, you will have to live like one of us.'

Meanwhile, in New Delhi, the director of the Information Bureau (IB), Raj Mitra, received a call on the secure line one afternoon. The voice on the other side was grim. 'There is a press secretary named Madhu Goyal in Islamabad. She seems to be exceptionally close to a certain Pakistani man who is twenty years younger than her.'

This was important information and, after mulling over it for a few minutes, Mitra summoned his personal assistant. 'Please check if the home secretary is in. I need to meet him urgently.'

'Yes, sir.'

His assistant was back in less than three minutes. 'Sir, the Secretary says you can meet him right now as the matter is urgent.'

Ten minutes later, Mitra was seated in the home secretary's office.

'Are you sure?' That was all he asked after Mitra briefed him about Madhu.

'Yes, my source is credible, sir. For the last few months, we have known that there is a mole in the Indian High

Commission who has been passing information on to the ISI [Inter-Services Intelligence]. But we never expected it to be our press secretary.'

'What's your plan of action, Mr Mitra?'

'I need to get to the bottom of the matter. At the same time, we need to be very careful.'

'You think we should inform our high commissioner?'

'No, sir. He need not be told at this stage. In fact, we should not involve anyone in the high commission in Islamabad as the word might get out to Madhu's handlers and the man she is meeting might go underground.'

'Hmm.'

'One wrong step and the situation could turn into a major fiasco. We will never know how much and what information she has passed on to him.'

'But we need to keep the chief of R&AW [Research and Analysis Wing] in the loop, right?'

'Of course.'

'Mr Mitra, I think we need answers to three questions. Correct me if I am wrong. One, what is the nature of the information that Madhu Goyal has passed on? Two, how much has she passed on? And three, who is this Pakistani man she is leaking information to?'

'Right, but there is a fourth question. Is Madhu really in love with this man who is twenty years younger than her? And we already know the answer to this question at least.'

The Secretary shifted in his chair. 'The answer is "yes". Mitra, this case has honeytrap written all over it. Has there ever been a case where an Indian woman has fallen prey to a honeytrap set by an officer of a foreign intelligence agency?'

'Never, sir. There have, however, been a handful of men, not just from the Indian intelligence services, but also from the armed forces, who have been compromised in this manner.'

After his meeting, Mitra returned to his office. He spoke to the R&AW chief on a secure line and right after, ordered two men from his counter-intelligence team to closely monitor Madhu.

Gradually, without taking the staff of the Indian High Commission into confidence, Mitra's team members started sending false information through Madhu to her lover. They were confident that as soon as the recipients of the information on the Pakistani side realized that it was wrong, they would get restless.

A month after the steady leak of false information started, Madhu was taken aback by Jamaal's behaviour one evening. They were in their usual room and had just finished a great session of sex.

'Who do you think you are? Why are you deliberately putting me into trouble?'

'What are you talking about?'

'You know very well what I'm talking about. You have been giving me wrong information of late. You are double-crossing me.'

Madhu didn't like this at all. First, there had been no agreement on how she would be required to behave after the wedding, and now this. She was no longer sure if Jammy really wanted to marry her. A thought crossed her mind— was she just being used? Is this nothing more than a younger Pakistani man wanting to have sex with an Indian woman?

Am I merely fulfilling some wicked fantasy? But she silently admonished herself for thinking such things. She was in a serious relationship and knew that relationships could be difficult, particularly in the beginning.

Jamaal looked at her and for the first time she couldn't read his expression. Was he trying to say something he was not allowed to? Whatever be the circumstances, she was sure he still loved her. He pulled her into an embrace. She melted in his firm grip. He began to kiss her passionately. Even as he was making love to her for the second time that evening, Madhu kept thinking about where she could have been at fault. She had done nothing wrong; she had passed on the information he had requested without worrying about her safety, without even thinking about what he would do with it. It was simple give and take. He loved her and she would go to any lengths to please him.

As was her way when she was worried about something, she decided to go on a long drive. After a restless night, Madhu left her house at sunrise. She had never worried about her safety and was used to driving alone. In fact, she had once driven all the way to Wagah border and crossed over into India.

She drove towards Lahore. On the way, she stopped at a KFC and ordered a burger and Coke. Back on the road, she tried to distract herself by humming songs from old Hindi films. By the time she drove into Lahore, it was early afternoon. She decided to visit her favourite bookstore.

The old shopkeeper recognized her. 'Madam, a few good spy novels have arrived. Would you like to see them?'

'Of course. Where are they?'

The shopkeeper pointed to a rack and Madhu selected four novels.

She thanked the shopkeeper, paid for the books and walked out. Still feeling restless, she decided to spend the night in Lahore. Madhu spent the entire evening in her hotel room. She finished one of the spy novels, ordered room service and slept around 11 p.m.

The next morning, she drove back to Islamabad. She couldn't stop thinking about her relationship. Jammy loved her a lot, of that she had no doubt, but she had no idea what he would do next. It was not just the fact that he was mercurial; Jammy's over-possessiveness was suffocating her.

She returned from Lahore on a Sunday. There was a small get-together planned at the Indian High Commission that same evening. As soon as she opened the door of her house, her phone started to ring. It was her colleague Asha.

'Madhu, where have you been? Are you joining us for the party this evening?'

'No. I'm not feeling well.'

'Oh! What happened?'

'Nothing too serious. I think it's just a cold and cough. A bit of fever too.'

'Please take care, but the boss said it was compulsory to attend the party.'

'I don't care for such rules made by the boss. Both of us know that he is an asshole.'

She heard her colleague giggle on the other side. No one liked the boss, but no one had the guts to call him names. Except Madhu, of course. Sometimes, when he sent her a message asking her to meet him in the office, she would ignore it.

Around 7 p.m., after a shower, Madhu poured herself a glass of red wine and settled down to read another of the spy novels that she had bought.

A week later, Madhu was ordered to go to New Delhi to help prepare for the South Asian Association for Regional Cooperation (SAARC) summit that was due to be held in a few months in Bhutan. She had not met Jammy since that distasteful evening when he had accused her of giving him false information. Her initial reaction to the trip to Delhi was that it was ill-timed as she had to sort out the situation with Jammy. But on second thoughts, she realized that a few days apart would do their troubled relationship good.

After landing in Delhi, she went to her home in Dwarka to meet her parents. She then got in touch with a few of her close friends and invited them over.

Sonia was the first to arrive. 'Oye, oye! You look like a pataka, yaar. Look at that glow.'

'Thank you, Sonia. You look wonderful too. How are you?'

Sonia sat on the sofa and smiled. 'I'm fine. Kids are settled, husband is busy, so all I do these days is shop.'

'Wow! Children settled! How time flies. Sometimes when I close my eyes, I can still recall our college days. The memories are so vivid.'

'Yes, so tell me, Madhu, when are you planning to settle down? You look so gorgeous, yaar, anyone would fall for you. Or do you already have somebody?'

Madhu thought of Jamaal and blushed. 'Arre, nahin. There is no one.'

Sonia spotted the lie, gave her a wink, and asked, 'Got it, so who is he?'

'No one, Sonia.'

'Swear on me there is no one.'

But Madhu was saved from answering as there was a knock on the door.

Three more of Madhu's friends had arrived, bouquets in hand, one of them holding a bottle of wine. They too, on Sonia's coaxing, tried their best to find out about Madhu's love interest. But she didn't tell anyone about Jamaal. Her lover was a Pakistani man and she would have to be careful about what she said.

The next morning, she went to the ministry of external affairs in South Block. As she sat, waiting to meet a senior officer, two policemen and a woman constable approached her.

'Yes?'

The inspector asked her, 'Are you Madhu Goyal?'

'Yes.'

'You are under arrest, Miss Madhu Goyal.'

'Are you out of your mind? I'm a diplomat. I have immunity from arrest. You are mistaken, Inspector.'

The inspector showed her the arrest warrant and took her into custody.

Since Madhu, an Indian diplomat posted in Pakistan, was arrested only a year and a half after the Mumbai attack of 2008, the media picked up the story immediately. Theories were floated, experts were invited to television studios to discuss the incident, and it wasn't long before the case took the nation by storm.

Two years later, in January 2012, the trial court framed charges against Madhu. Since she had already spent close to two years in Tihar Jail, she was granted bail. Soon after her release, Madhu said, 'I am innocent and the Indian High Commission in Islamabad has framed me in connivance with the Delhi Police.'

The investigations continued over the next few years. Initially, she was charged with Sections 3 and 5 of the Official Secrets Act (OSA), 1923, for lighter offences entailing a term of a maximum of three years. But later, more serious charges were included.

During the trial, the investigating officer said, 'After initially mocking the authorities, she cooperated with the team and gave access to her computer, mobiles and emails. The emails exchanged between Madhu and Jamaal formed the bulk of our charge sheet and have revealed, beyond doubt, that she was passing on information as asked due to her romantic association with Mr Jamaal.'

Finally, in May 2018, Madhu Goyal was convicted of spying for the ISI and awarded three years imprisonment. The more serious charges under the OSA, which entailed a term of up to fourteen years, were set aside by the court as none of the information that she had leaked pertained to the Indian defence organizations.

On the day of her final hearing, Madhu sat in the court, her hair well-groomed, an unreadable expression on her face as the judge announced the verdict. She remained calm.

After her conviction, Madhu looked around the crowded courtroom. Her eyes seemed to be searching for someone. It wasn't Jammy, as he had made no effort to communicate with her over the last several years. Perhaps she was trying to read the expressions of the people in the courtroom to make sense of it all. How was it that someone like her, a single woman who was also a senior citizen now, was not given any concession for her unblemished career, which spanned more than twenty-seven years?

The court rejected her appeal for leniency saying, 'Madhu is a modern, educated woman who had served in different embassies and, at the time of the offence, she was posted in a very sensitive position in the high commission.' They further added, 'Undoubtedly, from a person of her stature, it was expected that she would act in a more responsible manner than an ordinary citizen as she was at a high position of trust but her actions tarnished the image of the country and caused severe threat to the security of the country. Therefore, she does not deserve any leniency in punishment.'

The investigating officer later told the press, 'She blew the covers of all the Indian intelligence officials in Pakistan, disclosed biographical details of every employee at the high commission, and also mentioned the existence of "some secret routes to India".'

Madhu spoke to the media a few times and told her side of the story, but no one believed her.

While she was being escorted out of the courtroom, dozens of people from the media followed her, thrusting mikes into her face, but she ignored them all. Looking straight ahead, Madhu got into the waiting vehicle and, assisted by the police, was driven away.

Interesting information: In one of her emails, Madhu Goyal said that her lover, Jamaal, treated her like a dog. But in spite of this, she gave him all the information he demanded. Why did she do this? There are many theories, but the most likely reason is this: Madhu had always wanted to work with the diplomatic intelligence wing. She was very interested in espionage. But when her request was denied time after time, she decided to act like a spy and pass on information to whomsoever she pleased. It was her way of extracting revenge and, therefore, it was no surprise that when her house in Islamabad was searched, many espionage novels were found.

8

Cyanide Mallika

Chelamma's house was located in a village bordering
Bengaluru. It comprised two interconnected rooms where
she lived with her husband and three children.

That evening, it was dark by the time she returned home.
As she approached her house, her heart started to beat faster.
She owed several people a lot of money due to her failed chit
fund business and was scared that some of them would go to
her home and harm her children.

She pushed the door open and found her children
waiting. They ran towards her as soon as they saw her.

'Mom, food, give me food, I'm hungry.' The one who
spoke first was her youngest daughter. She was just two and
looked up at her mother through deep-set eyes. Clearly,
she was malnourished and her cheeks were glistening with
tears.

'Mom, where is the food?' The other two children, one
boy and one girl, three- and four-years-old respectively, asked
together.

Chelamma sat down heavily on the floor. 'There is no food today. I'm sorry.'

Through sobs, as the children clung to her, she added, 'I'll get food tomorrow morning, I promise, even if I have to kill someone.'

The door was thrown open just as she finished the sentence. Chelamma's husband, Kapalu, walked in. His eyes were bloodshot. As soon as his eyes fell on Chelamma, he charged towards her. Knowing what was coming next, she pushed the children away and got to her feet.

'You stupid woman!' He slapped her.

She staggered but found her balance. The youngest child started to cry.

'What did I do?' she shouted, defiance in her voice.

'What did I do?' her husband mimicked her and slapped her again. This time, she fell to the ground. The other two children also started to cry.

Kapalu turned towards the children. 'Stop.'

He vanished out of the door but was back in a minute. The four of them were too startled to move even an inch.

Kapalu beckoned to the eldest child. 'Krishna, take this and share it with everyone.'

He had a plastic bag in his hand, which he extended towards the boy. Krishna approached his father hesitantly, turned to look at his mother, and as she nodded, he took the bag and went to the other room. The other two children followed him without a word.

The husband and wife were alone in the room now. The man pulled up the only chair there and sat on it. Chelamma, who was on the floor, didn't move. The man's eyes were on her, while she stared at the floor.

Chelamma was around thirty. She was of medium build, had a dark complexion and black, curly hair that reached just below her shoulders. She and Kapalu had been married for eight years.

After a few minutes of silence, when Kapalu spoke, his voice was calmer. 'Why don't you stop this stupid chit fund thing if you can't make any money out of it?'

She didn't say anything and he continued, 'At least if you are at home, I don't have to worry about the children. You can cook for them and take care of the house.'

She looked up sharply. 'How much do you earn? You are just a tailor, not a king. I can't run the house with the money you make.'

'You can't run the house because you are greedy. How are the others managing, tell me?'

'I'm not just another person. I can earn.'

'You stupid fool, you are under debt. How much do you owe people?'

'I'm under debt, yes, but I will pay them back and I will earn a lot of money.'

'Why do you need so much money, Chelamma? Tell me, what do you desire?'

'I want a big house, a big car and servants working for us.'

'Are you mad? You think by getting all these things we will be happy? That's just a stupid idea. Money doesn't make people happy, family and love do.'

'Only money will make *me* happy,'

He got up again and picked up the stick that was placed against the wall next to the door. It was a bamboo stick, about three feet long. He had used it many times before. He swung it wildly and it caught Chelamma across her shoulders. A stinging pain shot through her body, but she didn't cry. She simply stared at him. The man hit her multiple times, but she didn't move. It was as if the pain receptors in her body were numb. Finally, when he got tired, he latched the door of the room in which the children were eating, removed her clothes, pulled down his pants and entered her. Five minutes later, he collapsed on top of her. Chelamma pushed him to one side and closed her eyes.

The next day, Chelamma woke up to a knock on the door. She peeped through a crack and sucked in a breath. Her worst fears had come true. The timing of this disaster was bad as her husband was yet to leave for work. She stepped out and closed the door behind her.

Ten people stood there, six men and four women. Chelamma knew precisely who they were and why they were there. Yet she asked, 'What do you want?'

The oldest amongst them, a man who appeared to be around sixty, spoke first. 'We want our money back.'

'I want to give your money back too, but you have to come to the office.'

Chelamma had hired a small room in a market six months ago when she had started her chit fund business. But for the past month, the room had been locked as she had nothing to give to the people who were asking for their investments to be returned.

The man's eyes narrowed as he said, 'Your office has been locked since last month.'

'Okay, listen, I'm not running away. I live here. My husband and children are right here. Why do you worry? I had invested most of our money in one company, but it deceived us.'

This time a woman who was around thirty spoke. 'We don't want to know who cheated you. We just want our money back.'

The door opened behind Chelamma. This was precisely what she didn't want. She stepped aside as her husband asked, 'What's this commotion about?'

'Your wife owes us money,' the old man said.

Chelamma's husband turned towards her. 'This is what I was talking about last night. How much do you owe these people?'

She didn't say anything. This was such an awkward question. She was not going to tell him in front of everyone how much she owed. If the word spread, then those who had been waiting patiently for their money would also join these people.

Her husband caught her ear and, twisting it, repeated the question.

Chelamma gasped in pain. 'Five lakhs.'

He let go of her ear. 'What? You bitch, you owe five lakh rupees? Where did all the money go?'

The people gathered in front of them started to get more agitated and began to close in.

Chelamma's husband slapped her. The old man raised his hand to slap her too, but brought his hand down. He said to her, 'We want the money by tomorrow morning. We don't want to know from where or how, we just want our money.'

The crowd began to disperse. Chelamma now breathed easy. She looked at her husband, not sure if he would slap her again or pull her in to have sex. He was looking down at her, his eyes red with anger, his body shaking. Finally, he did something that she had never imagined he would do.

'You can't live in this house any more. Get out! If I ever see you again, I swear, I will kill you.'

Chelamma wanted to feel anger or hatred for him, but she didn't feel anything. His words didn't mean anything. Her thoughts were clear: if I earn a lot of money, my husband will take me back and I will be reunited with my family.

She went inside the house, put her clothes into a small bag, peeped into the room where her children were sleeping and walked out. There were no tears, no remorse. She knew only one thing—that she was on a mission to make money.

Not sure where to go, Chelamma got into the first bus that arrived at the village bus stop. After half an hour, she got off, without even knowing the name of the stop.

She found herself in a desolate area. It was 10 a.m. and she was hungry and thirsty. She saw a small temple not far from where she stood. It was on a hillock and she could see whitewashed stairs leading to the top.

She walked to the foot of the hillock and began to climb. In ten minutes, she had reached the top. She turned and soaked in the scenery. In the distance, beyond the greenery, she could see a few high-rises. She was now closer to Bengaluru than she had ever been in her life. For some reason, this made her smile.

She turned her attention back to the temple. It was a small temple—a main building which had an idol of the deity placed inside and a few small rooms on one side. On the other side, she walked all around the main building to check, she noticed a few cattle in a shed. There was no human in sight.

Chelamma removed her chappals and entered the temple. The sanctum sanctorum had an idol of Lord Krishna. She folded her hands and began to chant mantras. Chelamma had always been fascinated by Sanskrit hymns and had memorized many of them. Her interest stemmed from her belief that if the gods were appeased, they would give her a lot of money.

Chelamma heard a sound and turned. A woman had entered the temple. She was accompanied by a man. Chelamma noticed that she was wearing a lot of gold jewellery. She wondered how much all that gold was worth. Could she somehow take the woman's jewellery and vanish? It was obviously not possible, she thought with frustration, as her attention shifted to the man. By now, both of them had folded their hands and their eyes were closed in prayer.

A priest appeared from behind the idol and showered rose petals on the couple. Then he looked at Chelamma, made a face, and threw a few on her as well. After finishing her prayers, Chelamma receded into the hall, away from the idol, and sat on one side on the floor, her eyes half closed and hands folded. She was trying to hear what the couple was saying to the priest. She soon learnt that the couple was childless and the priest had performed a special puja for them.

Before leaving, the couple handed over a Rs 1000 note to the priest as *dakshina* and pushed another Rs 1000 into the donation box. Then they were gone and the priest went inside too. He didn't even react to Chelamma's presence. She knew why. It was clear from her clothes and lack of jewellery that she was poor.

Chelamma once again went around the temple. This time, she found a few banana trees. In one of the banana bunches, she spotted a few ripe ones and since she could easily reach them when she raised herself on her toes, she plucked a few. After eating them, she stuffed a few more into her bag. After this, she took the whitewashed stairs down.

She was back at the bus stop. Once again, she had no destination in mind. All she knew was that she had to go where those tall buildings were.

By 3 p.m., she was in Bengaluru. She got off the bus in a locality called Koramangala. Since she had no money, she wanted a job that would provide her free food even if the salary was paid after a month.

In front of Chelamma was a housing society called Park View Residency. She stood at a little distance from the gate and started to observe it closely. Cars, in which sat women, and sometimes children, went in and out of the gate. All the women seemed rich to her, their skins soft, almost all of them fair-complexioned. Like milk, she whispered to herself.

Who worked for these people in their houses, she wondered? Within a few minutes, she knew the answer. While the drivers drove the cars that these rich people travelled in, women like Chelamma were walking in and out of the buildings. It was clear that these women worked for the families that lived there. After some time, Chelamma approached the guard who stood at the gate.

The guard spoke to her in a language that she had not heard before. She signalled with her hands that she could work and that she was in need of food.

The guard mistook her as someone who could cook. He asked for her ID. When she didn't understand him, he took out his own voter ID and showed it to her.

Chelamma was carrying her voter ID. She took it out of her purse and showed it to him. He took it and inspected it closely before returning it to her. Then he signalled for her to wait and reached for the intercom.

After ten minutes, another guard escorted her into a building and the two entered a lift. She had never seen a lift before and felt giddy. When they stepped out, the guard knocked on one of the two doors before them. It was opened by a woman who was around thirty.

'Cook.' That was all he said and left.

Chelamma had no clue what he had said and waited for the woman to speak. Fortunately for her, the woman invited her inside in a language that she understood.

'So, you are a cook?'

Chelamma nodded.

'Can you tell me since when you have been cooking?'

Chelamma was confused by the question but then realized that the guard must have misunderstood her gestures.

'Sorry, I have no experience in cooking. But if you give me a job, any job, I will learn and do it well.'

The woman's expression was unreadable. Finally, she said, 'Can you clean the house?'

'Yes.'

After a few basic questions about her family, the woman said, 'I will give you two thousand rupees to clean my house. Two visits, one in the morning and one in the evening. In the morning you clean utensils, mop the floor and wash clothes. In the evening, only wash utensils. Okay?'

Chelamma nodded. 'Yes, but I am very hungry. My husband threw me out of the house and I have not eaten since last night.'

She saw the woman's expression soften before it hardened again. 'What sort of man is your husband? Is he an alcoholic?'

Chelamma nodded even though her husband had never touched alcohol. She got pleasure in ruining his image. The bastard deserved it for what he had done to her.

The woman turned and disappeared into the house. Chelamma looked around the drawing room. It was one of the largest rooms she had ever seen. The sofa, the carpet, the paintings on the walls—it was as if she was standing in one of the rooms she had seen in the movies or on television. She could tell that the family living in the house was rich. Her mind started thinking about how she could make money off them.

The woman soon returned with a plate of rice and dal. There was some pickle on the side too. Chelamma sat on the carpet and ate gratefully as the woman sat on the sofa, watching her. When she had finished eating, Chelamma got up, followed the woman to a large kitchen, washed her plate and placed it near the sink. Then she turned and said, 'Thank you.'

After this, she closed her eyes and chanted a prayer in Sanskrit. When Chelamma opened her eyes, she saw that the woman had also closed her eyes.

As Chelamma stopped chanting, the woman opened her eyes. 'That was so soothing. So you also recite mantras?'

'Yes, I love bringing positive energy into the lives of people.'

'Thank you.'

'I don't have a place to live,' Chelamma said and started to cry.

The woman placed her hand on Chelamma's shoulder. 'You can stay in our house. We have a small room behind the kitchen.'

Chelamma was ecstatic.

Among all the tasks she did in the house in the following week, Chelamma soon realized that her employer valued her knowledge of mantras the most. She sometimes consulted Chelamma when there were guests at home and a discussion on the subject of rituals and mantras caused a difference of opinion. For the first time in her life, Chelamma realized the power she had because of her knowledge of mantras.

In her spare time, she started to observe the cook. Once she was confident that she had learnt enough, she confided to her employer one evening, 'Madam, when I told you that I didn't know how to cook, I didn't know what your family ate. But now I want to tell you that I can cook better than your cook.'

The woman had taught her to address her as 'madam'. She had also taught her a few basic words of English. The same day, she fired her cook and Chelamma was promoted. Another woman was hired the next day to do the cleaning.

The family Chelamma worked for had three members. The woman's husband worked long hours and was away from 7 a.m. till 10 p.m. The couple also had a four-year-old son.

In just a few days, Chelamma was fed up of cooking. She had to keep preparing fresh food all day long as everyone ate at different times.

One morning, while the child was at school and the husband at office, the woman said, 'Chelamma, I'm going out for half an hour.'

She locked the house from outside. As soon as Chelamma was alone, she entered her employers' bedroom and started to go through the cupboard. She had opened the cupboard once before, when the woman was taking a bath. At that time, she had found a bundle of five-hundred-rupee notes. She had pulled out ten notes from the bundle and returned the rest.

This time, she found two bundles inside the cupboard. Both were of five-hundred-rupee notes. She pulled out ten notes from each and was about to close the cupboard when greed got the better of her. She pulled out five more notes from each bundle before gently closing the cupboard. After she had returned to the kitchen, she heard the sound of the front door opening. The woman had returned.

Chelamma could hear footsteps right behind her. Clearly, the woman had returned with someone else.

Chelamma turned and saw two guards standing on either side of the woman.

'You thief! Give me my money back!'

Chelamma was stunned. How had she found out? The guards moved towards her. It was time for action. She charged at the men with all her force, her head bent.

The impact surprised the men and in the confusion she ran outside, shouting, 'Help, help!'

She used the stairs and kept running till she reached the gate. There was another guard there, blocking her path.

'Help, help,' she shouted and the man looked behind her. In those few seconds she was out of the gate. She was barefoot but that was the last thing on her mind as she raced on the hot concrete.

It was 11 a.m. After a few minutes, she stopped and looked back. There was no one chasing her. She had outrun them. She was relieved.

She saw a park nearby and entered it. There she found a bench and sat down heavily on it. She soon realized that there were two things she couldn't do. First, she couldn't go back to her husband's house ever again as her employers would certainly notify the local police and give them the address from her voting card. And second, she could no longer use her name.

After she got her nerve back, she smiled. She still had Rs 15,000. Even though she had left her bag in the house, all it had was a few saris and some odds and ends. She put a hand into her blouse where she had hidden the money and touched it. Her smile widened.

An hour later, she walked out of the park, her palm covering her face, head slightly bent and glanced around. All was quiet. A bus came to a halt a few feet away. She saw her chance and, after one final glance around, boarded the bus.

Chelamma bought a ticket for the final destination. Forty minutes later, she got off at a small terminal. There were people milling about and there was a cigarette vendor in one corner. She walked outside the terminal. Alongside the road were all kinds of shops: a tea shop with bunches of bananas hanging outside, sari showrooms, an Udupi restaurant and a jewellery shop. Her eyes were drawn to the jewellery shop. The banner outside had a picture of a beautiful woman flaunting gold jewellery on her neck, ears, hair, nose, fingers and wrists. She imagined the woman without the ornaments and made a face. Without all that gold, the woman would not be beautiful. Plain like her, perhaps.

'Ah gold!' she exclaimed.

She walked into the shop and was greeted sceptically by the sales staff behind the counter. She knew why. They probably thought she was too poor to buy any jewellery.

'I want to buy a nice pair of earrings.'

A man pulled out a tray from behind the counter and showed her some earrings.

'How much do these cost?'

'One thousand each.'

'What? How are they so cheap? Are they fake?'

The man crossed his arms as the other sales staff looked on with interest. 'No, these are not fake, but they are gold-plated.'

'I want only solid gold.'

The man looked at the others before turning around to open a cupboard. He now pulled out another tray.

'These are pure gold. Prices start from ten thousand.'

Chelamma tried all twenty pairs of earrings on the tray. She could see the doubt on the faces of the sales staff because they were confident that she didn't have the money to buy such expensive earrings.

Finally, she selected a pair. 'I want to buy these.'

'Those are for twelve thousand.'

She pulled the money out of her blouse, counted out Rs 12,000 and tucked the rest back in. The man took the money and started to wrap the earrings.

As she was waiting, another man approached her from behind the counter. She guessed that he was the owner.

'Madam, that's a lot of money. I know it's not my business, but may I know from where you got so much money?'

Chelamma's first reaction was anger. If she had a knife, she would have slit his throat. But she smiled and said, 'My husband threw me out of the house. This is all the money that I have. I had been waiting for the last five years for him to gift me some gold, but he never did. He only loves to drink.'

The owner's face was clouded with concern. 'Oh, I'm sorry to hear this.'

'I know this is all the money I have, but today is my wedding anniversary. If I buy gold and pray with all my heart, I am sure my husband will take me back.'

The owner fumbled for words before he finally said, 'Gold brings good luck, fortune and happiness, that's right, but what if he doesn't take you back? I think you should save this money.'

'What sort of a shopkeeper are you? Are you denying a sale?'

'Yes, but for your good.'

Chelamma closed her eyes and began to chant a prayer. She didn't move for five minutes. When she finally opened her eyes, everyone was looking at her, the expressions on their faces uncertain.

'I will buy the earrings. God will protect me.'

The salesman handed her the earrings, which he had put in an attractive bag. She removed them from the bag, wore them and marched out.

Realizing that she was hungry, she entered the Udupi restaurant she had spotted earlier and ate a plate of idli and vada. Then she admired her reflection in a mirror facing her table and smiled. She looked beautiful and that lifted her spirits. But soon she was depressed again as she remembered that she was all by herself with no place to live, no job and little money.

After walking the streets for several hours, she once again found herself in front of the jewellery shop. After some thought, she went inside and began to cry loudly. She was no longer wearing the earrings.

'What happened, what happened?' The owner approached her. A salesman brought her a glass of water.

She let the suspense build as she kept wailing. Finally, she raised her head and through her tears explained the problem. 'I prayed at the temple on my way back home. I showed my husband the gold earrings and thought he would be happy. But after taking the earrings, he once again kicked me out of the house. I now have no place to go and no money.' She started to cry again.

The owner said, 'Don't cry please. Your husband is inhuman. Don't you have relatives with whom you could stay for a few days?'

'I don't have any place to go. He has poisoned everyone's mind against me. Everyone thinks I am a witch. Do I look like a witch to you?'

'No. I think you should go to the police.'

'Sir, I am an Indian wife. I would never go to the police and cause harm to my husband. I'm his wife, how could you even say that?'

The mild admonishment in her voice stopped the man from saying anything further.

Finally, Chelamma said, 'Can I work here? I will clean the shop, do anything you want me to do. Then after a few days I can go back to my husband. Maybe God will put some sense into him. I will pray every day.'

After some thought the man said, 'What's your name?'

'Laxmiamma.'

'Look, Laxmiamma, I really want to help you, but we already have someone who cleans the shop.'

'I can do anything. Anything you want.'

The owner finally agreed to employ her as a workshop assistant.

The workshop was on the first floor and guarded by a metal grill door. He took her there. The man opened the grill door and knocked on a second door. A wiry man opened it. They stepped inside. Three people were at work.

'This is Laxmiamma. She will help with all the cleaning.'

The owner left and the man who had opened the door explained the duties to her. 'Here, take these crystals.'

She took a small glass beaker from him. Next, he gave her a cloth and a few nuggets of what looked like rough stones.

'Do you know what these are?' he asked, pointing to the stones.

'Stones,' she replied. That got the three men laughing.

'These are pieces of raw gold. We have to use these crystals and that cloth to clean them and make them shine.'

She nodded as the man continued, 'And do you know what these crystals are?'

She shook her head.

'That's potassium cyanide. Ever heard of it?'

She shook her head again.

'It's a poison. The world's deadliest poison. Anyone who takes even a spoonful will die in a few minutes. Therefore,' he held out a pair of gloves, 'use these. If you have even a small cut on your hands, this poison can be fatal.'

She nodded and sat down. The wiry man placed the items before her.

'Can I rest for a few minutes first?' she asked him.

'Yes, today is your first day, take your time. This is not an easy job. Most people don't last more than a few days.'

Chelamma rested her back against the wall and closed her eyes. The first face she saw was of her husband. It would be so wonderful if she could kill her husband with a spoonful of the poison. She would then be able to reclaim her life and be reunited with her children.

At the end of the day, the owner came to her and said, 'The shop is closed now. We have to seal the workshop. You go down and eat something. Then you can sleep. We will be back by eight in the morning. By then, I want the shop cleaned, the stairs cleaned, the area outside the workshop cleaned, and you should have finished your breakfast and bath. Okay?'

Chelamma quickly left the shop, ate some rice and sambar from a nearby stall and then returned. The owner was ready to leave and so were the sales and the workshop staff.

After they had locked her in, she casually looked around. There was a lot of gold in the shop, but everything was locked in sturdy cupboards that were built into the walls. By now, she had guessed how her erstwhile employer had found out that she had stolen money. She had been monitoring her through cameras. Chelamma was sure that there were cameras in the shop as well and that someone could be watching her. She therefore pulled out the mattress that had been given to her and lay down to sleep.

The next few days passed quickly. Chelamma kept her attraction for gold under check and focused on her work. But as she got comfortable with the place and the staff, she started to get ideas.

However, she was soon faced with another dilemma. She learnt that the owner donated a lot of money to charities and orphanages. This earned him her respect and she decided that she would do no harm to such a nice human being.

A few months later, one night when she was alone, she got an idea. 'What if,' she whispered to herself, 'I stole some of the cyanide and used it to steal gold from other people?'

Over the next few weeks, the idea took root in her mind.

Finally, ten months after she was hired, it was time for her to make a move. She told the owner one morning as soon as he arrived, 'My husband came here yesterday.'

'When? Why didn't you introduce me to him?'

'I'm sorry. He came when I was eating lunch at the cart where I eat every day. He is feeling guilty. He misses me a lot and wants me back.'

'So?'

'I have decided to quit and go back home.'

'Are you out of your mind, Laxmiamma? What if he starts beating you again?'

'No, he won't.'

She was holding a small cloth bag in which were all her belongings—a few saris, some undergarments, a towel, a couple of pairs of chappals and a shawl.

'Please take care,' was all the owner finally said.

Chelamma thought his eyes were moist. But hers were dry. She was starting out on a new mission. And this time, she had a foolproof plan.

She went to a famous temple not far from the shop. Inside her bag she also had about half a kilo of potassium cyanide, which she had stolen in small quantities over a period of several months.

In the temple, she spent almost two hours looking for devotees and was left wondering how she would use the cyanide to kill anyone before she stole their gold. There were cameras everywhere, policemen in uniform near the gates, and also too many people who could chase a thief in minutes. By that night, she had visited three other temples in Bengaluru and got the same feeling.

The failure of her plan was imminent. Her idea of poisoning devotees who were wearing a lot of gold and robbing them didn't seem practical. It was a huge blow.

But there had to be a way, she thought. If not in Bengaluru, then somewhere else, where the temples were not as crowded.

She took an autorickshaw to the bus depot and scanned the destinations of the intercity buses. A bus that was about to leave was headed to Tirupati. She bought a ticket and settled into a window seat. When a woman came and sat next to her, she asked, 'How much time does it take to get to Tirupati?'

'Five hours.'

Chelamma didn't like the sound of that. She was not prepared to travel such a long distance. Meanwhile, the bus started to move. Within half an hour, Bengaluru had been left behind. The wind that came rushing in through the open window was cooler now. It was the October of 1999.

After an hour, the bus halted at a stop that read 'Hoskote'. On the way into the small town, Chelamma had noticed a temple that looked deserted. She decided to get off the bus.

She walked for about half an hour and by sunset she was at the temple. She went inside, removed her sandals and stepped on the small marble exterior. Inside, she saw a woman praying. There was no one else. She went and stood close to the woman, glanced at her discreetly and then closed her eyes. The woman was wearing a lot of gold.

Chelamma opened her eyes a crack and observed that there was no one in sight. There were several lit diyas set out on a thali. This meant that the priest was somewhere around. She started to mumble prayers, just loud enough for the woman to hear. As she sensed the woman moving away, Chelamma finished her prayers too and turned, 'Madam?'

The woman stopped to look at her. 'I'm not madam. My name is Roshini.'

'Oh, I am sorry. I am from Bengaluru where women of high status have to be addressed as "madam".'

'But I am not a woman of high status. I am just like you.'

By now Chelamma had reached close to her and said, 'But you look so rich—look at all the gold you are wearing.'

'Oh this,' the woman smiled as she touched her necklace. 'Not all of these ornaments are mine; some belong to my mother-in-law. The priest asked me to wear as much gold as I could for the ritual.'

'Oh!' Chelamma began to process the information.

'But the priest is not here. So, I am going back.'

'Sister, what problem are you facing?'

'It is my husband's health. The doctors have given up; only God can save him now they say.'

Chelamma smiled. She had figured out a plan. 'You know, sister, I am an expert in such rituals.'

'Really? Can you help me?'

'Yes. All that is needed is a thirty-minute mandala puja, which I can do right here.'

'Thank you. What do I have to do?'

'Nothing. Tell me, have you had a bath?'

'Yes.'

'This means your body is clean. Now I will give you some holy water to cleanse your insides and once you drink that I will chant mantras. That's all.'

The woman started to look doubtful. Chelamma knew she had to act quickly.

She pulled out a steel glass from her bag and walked across to a tap nearby. There she filled the glass with water and, as her back was turned towards the woman, she put two spoonfuls of cyanide into the water.

When she turned around, the woman was looking towards the exit. Chelamma quickly approached her and took out a bed sheet and a potato from her bag. She spread the bed sheet out on the ground and sat down, signalling the woman to do the same. The woman kept standing, now even more befuddled, her fingers continually fiddling with the end of her pallu.

Chelamma took out a bundle of incense sticks, pulled out a few and lit them. She stuck them into the potato and, as the smoke began to curl up, she said in a soothing voice, 'Amma, please sit down. I'm not even demanding a fee. Give me whatever dakshina you wish. I only want to help you.'

The woman, perhaps realizing that all these preparations had been done for her and it would now be rude to walk away, sat down hesitantly. Chelamma smiled and picked up the steel glass.

'Here, drink this and we can start immediately.'

The woman took the glass and slowly drank the water. Since cyanide dissolves completely and has no odour, she didn't spot anything amiss.

Now, Chelamma knew, it would only be a matter of minutes. Even though she had never administered cyanide to anyone, she had seen enough movies to know how it worked. She knew, therefore, that the woman would fall unconscious in three to five minutes. She looked around to see if anyone else had come into the temple. There was no one. There was no sign of the priest either.

Chelamma smiled and asked the woman to close her eyes. As she obeyed, Chelamma started chanting. Two minutes later, the woman opened her eyes and said, 'I'm not feeling well. I have to go.' She tried to get to her feet but fell down.

The woman had by now realized that there was something seriously wrong with her. She looked at the empty glass and opened her mouth to shout for help. Chelamma jumped up and put her hand across the woman's mouth. The woman struggled, but her resistance quickly weakened. In less than a minute she was unconscious, her face red.

This was the time. Chelamma acted quickly. She removed the woman's gold ornaments and vanished from the temple. The robbery gave her such a high that she ran like never before.

She reached the bus stop, took a bus back to Bengaluru and got off on the city's outskirts. She rented a small room in a lodge and slept. The next morning she left the lodge by 8 a.m.

By evening, she had sold the gold for Rs 1 lakh to a goldsmith. It was a small shop with just one person. The shopkeeper had asked her just once, 'Where did you get this from?'

'You want it or not?'

The man gave her Rs 1 lakh. It was so much money that Chelamma didn't even ask him how much the gold was worth. This time, she found a better lodge to spend the night in.

For the next few weeks, she closely followed the newspapers. A search was conducted, but since no one had seen her, the police reached a dead end. The case taught her an important lesson: she would have to be more careful next time—one wrong step and it would all be over.

After a month, Chelamma found employment as a cook. She decided to focus only on her job for a while.

The house she was working in belonged to a wealthy family. A very wealthy family. The woman was a housewife and her husband worked in a big company in Bengaluru. They had two sons, both in their teens, and the man's parents also lived with them. Chelamma was not the only cook. There was a younger girl who assisted her. But even with her help, Chelamma found the work back-breaking.

Within three months, she realized that the family had a lot of gold. Although she had decided not to rob any more, on her worst days, her thoughts did drift. Chelamma had already boasted to the woman that she knew a lot about rituals.

One day, when her husband was at work, the children were at school and her in-laws were away on a week-long religious tour, the woman asked Chelamma to help her plan a puja.

'Next week,' she said, 'after my in-laws are back, I have invited the priest to come and perform a puja.'

'That's very nice,' said Chelamma with a smile.

'Can you help me with the preparations?'

'Yes, what do you want to know?'

'The priest told me to wear gold jewellery. Can you help me decide how much is enough?'

'Yes, madam.'

With this, the woman went into her bedroom. Chelamma followed her. Inside, the safe was already open and there were many sets of gold jewellery laid out on the bed.

'Which ones do you think will make the God happiest?'

Chelamma's eyes widened at the sight of so much gold. Her first instinct was to hit the woman and run off with the gold. But she knew she couldn't be lucky every time. So, she checked herself and smiled. 'Let me see.'

Finally, she selected a few ornaments. 'I think these would be nice.'

The woman smiled. 'Thank you.'

By now, the sight of all the gold had weakened Chelamma's resolve.

'Wait, I will be right back.' Chelamma went to the kitchen and sent the young girl to get some chilli power. After the girl left, she went to her room and stuffed all her belongings into her bag. Then she put the bag near the front door. She then returned to her employer's bedroom. Chelamma felt the same high that she had experienced after the kill in the Hoskote temple.

By now, the woman had put most of the gold back into the safe. As she turned, Chelamma, who had picked up a rolling pin from the kitchen, hit her on the head with all the power she had. The woman's eyes rolled back and she slumped to the floor.

The safe was yet to be locked. Chelamma picked up as much gold as she could hold in both her hands and ran towards the door. She stuffed the jewellery into her bag and dashed towards the door. Her employers lived in a bungalow and all she had to do now was to tackle the guard. The guard saw her coming and realized from her expression that something was wrong. He shouted for her to stop. Chelamma didn't and continued running towards the wrought-iron gates as fast as she could.

The guard jumped on her and both fell to the ground. Chelamma screamed in pain as she skidded on the cemented driveway, grazing her knees and elbows. She managed to get back on her feet quickly and jumped towards the partially open gate before the guard could recover. Just then, the gate was pushed further open and the girl who helped her in the kitchen walked in, oblivious to the commotion. The swinging gate caught Chelamma unawares and she lost her balance, falling once more on her knees and elbows. This time, her bag flew out of her hands.

'Stop her!' shouted the guard.

Together, the guard and the girl jumped on Chelamma. Soon, hearing the noise, people started to gather on the road.

The police were there fifteen minutes later and Chelamma was arrested.

Her employer received a few stitches, but she recovered in a few days.

A month later, in October 2000, Chelamma was convicted based on the statements of the witnesses and the proof provided by the gold that was found in her bag. She was given six months in jail.

The jail term broke her. She missed her children and decided to never get involved in any criminal activity. Whenever she thought about the woman she had murdered in Hoskote, she shivered. She was so lucky to have escaped. If the police ever found out, she would be given the death sentence. But these changes were only in her conscious mind. Deep inside, she began to see the killing and the fact that she had escaped arrest as a big win.

After she was released from jail, she went back to her village but found her home locked. She tried her best to identify the whereabouts of her children, but there were no leads. No one seemed to know where her family had moved.

Once again, family-less, she returned to Bengaluru and started to work in a house as a cook. This time, she introduced herself as Parvathiamma. She worked in several houses from 2000 to 2007 without committing any crime. Though she helped many of her employers in performing rituals, she was never swayed by her greed for their gold.

All was going well, until in 2007 a memory came back to her. After she had murdered the woman in Hoskote in 1999, she had buried the remaining cyanide under a tree. Instead of simply discarding it, she had dug a small hole using the steel glass, around a foot in depth, and placed the plastic bag with the cyanide inside it. Then she had covered it with the loose soil and stamped on it till it was flat.

Now, almost eight years later, she began to worry about that cyanide. What if an animal, a goat or a cow, dug it up and consumed it? She felt sad at the thought and knew that she needed to do something about it. Finally, she decided to go back to Hoskote.

One day, she took a bus to Hoskote. She didn't ask the driver to stop as the bus crossed the temple. She did exactly what she had done the first time. After getting off the bus at the designated stop, she walked back towards the temple. On the way, she spotted the tree. It had hardly changed. She walked up to it and tried to locate the spot where she had buried the poison. But there were no reference points to guide her.

It was noon and there was no one in sight. She had brought a small shovel with her. She began to dig in the most probable spots. Finally, after a dozen or so attempts, she found the plastic bag. Careful not to damage it, she first cleared the soil around it and then pulled it out to inspect its contents. The white power was exactly as it was when she had buried it. No animal had pulled it out.

Chelamma carefully put the plastic pouch in her bag. She thought of disposing it of in a pond. But what about the fish, her inner voice asked?

Not knowing what to do, she returned to Bangalore with it. By now she was living in a tiny one-room house. Not living with her employers gave her some time to herself.

She sat in a chair, the plastic packet at her feet, and looked out the window. She could see colourful buildings not far away. Cars went past on a road close to her house and music floated in from a building nearby. Everyone, it seemed, was rich, happy and successful. Everyone except her.

By morning, she had made up her mind. She needed money; she had to be rich enough to buy a car and a house and to do what she pleased. Soon, with a small portion of the cyanide in her bag, she was on the prowl once again.

From October to December 2007, in less than three months, Chelamma killed six more women. Her modus operandi didn't change much from her first murder, except that now she scouted for targets in one temple and convinced them to come to another temple for a special puja. She deliberately chose the second temple on the outskirts of Bengaluru, one that she had visited earlier and found to be desolate.

Her victims were all desperate women who had turned to God for an answer. One was a childless woman, one longed for a male child, one was searching for her granddaughter, another wanted a cure for chronic asthma and one was a priest who wanted Chelamma to sponsor a minor renovation in a temple.

When the victims arrived at the deserted temple, Chelamma would be ready with cyanide-laced water and food items. It was not difficult for her to convince them to partake of the 'holy' items before the puja.

With each success, she grew bolder. She sold most of the jewellery to different shops and made plenty of money. She now had several lakh of rupees in her house and started to flaunt some of the gold that she had stolen. She also bought expensive saris and travelled only in taxis.

On 31 December 2007, Chelamma had just sold a big consignment and was waiting at a bus stop when she was approached by four policemen. It was after sunset and she had decided against taking a taxi as she had a lot of money in her purse. Public transport was a safer option.

'Are you Swapnamma?'

The policeman took the name that she had been using of late.

She nodded.

'We want to search your bag.'

One of the policemen took it from her before she could object. He emptied the contents on to the ground. Gold ornaments were the first to fall out, followed by bundles of five- and one-hundred-rupee notes.

By now, a crowd had started to gather. Cars began to slow down too.

'Where did you get all this from?'

Chelamma remained silent, her mind numb. What was happening? She knew she had to do something. But the only thing that came to her mind was to run away. But how could she run away from all the wealth on the ground? It was her property.

Chelamma had no clue that her first murder case in Hoskote was closed as there were no witnesses and no proof. But when she started to commit murder after murder, and all the victims were killed in temple premises in a similar manner, the police formed two crack teams. While one started to keep a watch on desolate temples outside the city, the second team sounded all the goldsmiths in the area. Finally, one of the goldsmiths that Chellamma sold the gold to informed the police as soon as she left.

Chelamma was arrested. It took the police only a day before she admitted to all the killings. Within a few months, the police had prepared a watertight case against her.

Chelamma was finally convicted of six cold-blooded murders and awarded the death sentence.

The media gave her a new name: Cyanide Mallika. Mallika was one of the names she had used. Later, her death sentence was reduced to life imprisonment.

Interesting fact: While in jail after her sentencing, Chelamma learnt that a serving chief minister's top political aide was lodged in the same jail. She insisted on meeting her, saying she was very fond of the chief minister and her aide, even though she had never met them. Her request was denied of course.

9

The Serial Killer's Girlfriend

At first, Leena Aulakh didn't believe it. She had always known that she was beautiful, but being crowned a beauty queen at a glittering ceremony in Chandigarh on that September day in 1995 was a different experience altogether.

The announcer's voice was still echoing in her ears as she stood on the stage, bathed in the brilliant glow of artificial lights. She had butterflies in her stomach and her head was spinning with the thunderous applause. Behind her stood more than twenty models, shocked at the announcement but maintaining their smiles. She knew that many of those girls didn't like her. But now it did not matter. She was beautiful and here was proof.

A woman approached her, bearing a crown on a tray. The previous year's beauty queen placed it on her head. Leena felt weightless.

The announcer was back on. 'Congratulations to Leena Aulakh from Ludhiana, the new Miss Chandigarh! Give her a big round of applause.'

Thousands of people began clapping.

The announcer continued, 'And isn't this girl beautiful?'

The audience hooted.

'Have you ever seen a more beautiful girl?'

'Nooooo,' the crowd shouted.

After the first and second runners-up were felicitated, the event was over. Leena was escorted to the car that was waiting for the winner. A few tough-looking security men appeared by her side as she walked, keeping her just-formed fans at bay. She stopped, turned towards them and blew them a kiss. The fans went crazy.

Ten minutes later, as the car rolled into the porch of the hotel that the organizers had booked her into for the next two days, Leena could see that the press was already waiting with their cameras and scribble pads. As soon as she placed one long, high-heeled leg out of the car, the flashes started popping. She emerged as elegantly and as deliberately as she could, soaking in the moment, walking towards the entrance.

Somewhere in those few moments a star was born, a star who would do anything, including murder and looting, just to keep her image alive.

After freshening up, she was escorted to the hotel's lawns where a special announcement party had been organized. She met people, signed autographs and gave a short speech. This was her new life. Leena Aulakh, the daughter of a college professor and a schoolteacher from Ludhiana, had finally arrived on the big stage.

'Oh my God! I have never seen a more beautiful woman in my life,' said a man.

She turned towards him. 'Thank you.'

'You are so pretty, Leena ji. Wow!' said another man.

'Thank you.'

'Madam, you should be Miss Universe,' said a third man.

'Thank you.'

And the praise continued.

She drank wine for the first time in her life, nibbled on exotic finger food and had a sit-down dinner with some very important guests. The social status of the men and women seated at her table was so high that had it not been for her label of Miss Chandigarh, they would never have spoken to her. But now, she was their equal.

She ate delicately and put to use the table manners that all the finalists had been taught by the organizers.

Later that night, back in her room, she took a warm bath, drank some more wine from the bottle that was in the minibar and called her mother. 'Mom?'

'Congratulations, my darling daughter. We saw it on TV.'

'Thank you, mom.'

'When will you be back home, beta?'

'Soon, mom, soon.'

She wished her mother goodnight and lay on the bed, soon falling asleep. That night, Leena's dreams took her to a far-off land, a land where she belonged, where people paid money just to get a glimpse of her. She was beautiful, and now she was a beauty queen.

The next day was as delightful as the previous one. Her handler till such time as she stayed at the hotel, Samrat Singh, came to her room at 9 a.m. and briefed her on her engagements for the day.

'Madam, there are a few photo shoots for interviews. The designers have already brought the dresses. As soon as you are ready, I will send them to your room, one by one. Then there's a TV interview after lunch, and later in the evening, there is a cocktail party to which celebrities have been invited.'

Leena had by now finished her breakfast in bed. She smiled at him. He was around twenty, six feet tall and had a seriousness about him that Leena found attractive.

Can I just get up and pull him into bed, she wondered?

'Oh, that's a lot of work to do in one day. Can you cut out some of my appointments?' she said, to tease him.

She saw his face cloud with concern and his eyebrows knit together. The desire to pull him into bed became even stronger.

'I'm sorry, madam, let me see what I can do.'

'Arre, I was just teasing you. The programme is fine. Why are you so serious?'

He smiled and that ruined it. The smile didn't suit him and Leena no longer found him as desirable as she had a moment ago. He was just another ordinary man. There would be plenty of rich and interesting people to interact with at the party that evening.

During the cocktail party, almost everyone she spoke to said the same thing. 'Leena, you are gorgeous, you should be in the film industry.'

That decided it for her. When it was time for her to leave Chandigarh, she didn't return to Ludhiana, but flew first to Delhi and onward to Mumbai, where she had decided she would make a new life for herself. She was meant to be rich, successful and desired by millions.

In Mumbai, she checked into a five-star hotel and began to plan her course of action. She had no contacts and didn't know how to land roles in the industry. But she knew one thing for certain. Modelling was the easiest route to being noticed. If she could become a successful model, she would make the right contacts. She already had a brilliant start in Chandigarh and all she had to do now was to keep at it.

Within a few hours of her arrival, she had identified the top two modelling agencies in Mumbai. While one was in Andheri, the other was in Juhu, both not far from her hotel. She visited the agencies the following morning and received the same response: 'We need a fresh portfolio.'

Though she had got a portfolio made in Ludhiana, on the basis of which she had been called for the pageant in Chandigarh, she now needed a better one.

She asked the staff at the second agency, 'Can you help me get in touch with a professional? You see, I am new here in Mumbai.'

'Sure,' the man nodded and wrote down a number on a piece of paper and gave it to her.

She called the number and someone called Romi D'souza answered the phone. A meeting was fixed for 10 a.m. the following morning. She now had the entire day to shop for clothes.

Leena had plenty of cash thanks to the prize money she had received. She shopped for a few dresses and accessories and was pleased with her purchases. But she also needed the right make-up and so she called the photographer once again. 'I need a make-up person for tomorrow too.'

'Of course, my service includes make-up.'

'No, I don't want just any make-up person. I want to hire the best. Can you share a number?'

There was a pause on the other side before the photographer said, 'Sure, please note this number down . . .'

Shopping done, make-up and photographer all sorted for the next day, Leena looked around. Opposite her was an upscale restaurant. It was 3 p.m. and just the sight of it made her realize that she was hungry. The breakfast that she had eaten at the hotel had long been digested.

She entered the restaurant and was welcomed by a waiter who escorted her to a table.

'Welcome, madam. Here is the menu.'

The waiter gave her the menu card and moved away. He stood at a little distance and waited for her to decide. The restaurant was almost empty; just one other table was occupied by a couple. From where she sat, Leena could see the sea and the swaying coconut trees that lined the beach. It looked pretty.

She turned to look at the waiter and he was quick to come to her side. 'Get me some wine.'

'Yes, madam,' he bowed. 'Which one?'

'Which one is good here?'

'Can I get you the one that I like the most?' there was a hint of a smile on his face.

'Sure,' Leena smiled encouragingly.

The man vanished.

He was back in a few minutes with a bottle, which he held out so she could check the temperature and the brand. Leena had no idea about wines, so she just placed her hand on the bottle to check if it was chilled and nodded.

He poured her a glass and waited till she took a sip. Leena smiled. She was not sure if it was good or bad. It tasted similar to the wine she had had at the hotel in Chandigarh.

'It's really good.'

'Thank you, madam.' With this, the waiter vanished again.

Leena had a few sips and soon her thoughts turned to her photo shoot scheduled for the next day. She decided to eat quickly and return to her hotel so that she could sleep early and wake up looking her best.

The waiter was back again and this time he was holding a plate. He placed it in front of her. It was a platter of olives, cheese and nuts.

'This is complimentary, madam.' The smile was obvious this time.

His smile was infectious and Leena found herself smiling too.

'Thank you,' she picked up an olive.

'Madam, can I say something?'

She looked at him. He was attractive. But his accent was a bit strange.

'Sure.' Leena picked up a piece of cheese and washed it down with a sip of wine.

'I have a hobby. I like to guess the backgrounds of the people who come into the restaurant. For most, I just guess but don't have the courage to ask. But with you, I feel comfortable asking if my guess is right or wrong.'

'Okay, tell me who I am.'

'You are from Delhi or somewhere close to Delhi. You are a model and you are here to make a career in Bollywood.'

This was bang on target and she didn't know what to say.

'Am I right?'

'Almost, except that I am not from Delhi. I am from Ludhiana.'

'Don't ask me to guess your name, because I can't do that.'

'It's Leena Aulakh.'

'And my name is Sanjay Ranade.'

She then told him about the photo shoot and he invited her to have lunch at the restaurant after it was done. She agreed and, after eating her meal, left.

The photo shoot was a mind-blowing experience. In just three hours, the photographer took almost 200 pictures of her in five different outfits. By 3 p.m., she was back at the restaurant.

Leena had no idea that the chance meeting with Sanjay would become both the boon and bane of her life. Over the next few weeks, from being friends, the two became lovers.

They would go for long walks on the beach after Sanjay's shift. They ate together, laughed and watched movies holding hands and kissed in the dark.

One evening, after sex, Sanjay said, 'I think we need to do something. I've spent all my money. How about you?'

'I'm almost done too.'

'Is there someone who can loan you some money? My father was in the army. Now that he has retired, he gets a small pension with which he barely manages the house. If I ask him for money, he will be very upset because he expects me to earn and support him.'

'The situation is slightly different for me. My parents don't need money from me, but I can't ask them for money either.'

'Yaar, people in Mumbai have so much money and here we are, penniless. Don't you think it's unfair?'

'Yes, it is. But what can we do?'

'That is precisely what I am asking.'

The next week, Leena called everyone she had sent her portfolio to, but there was no positive response. There were no offers for a role in a film, or for television, and no leads for ad-films either. A beautiful girl with no money and no job, she felt trapped and on the edge like the millions who had failed before her. But Leena refused to give up. She started dropping hints to the people who mattered that she believed in the casting couch. Even though that brought her close to a few producers and directors, they never kept the promises they made in bed.

One day, she declared, 'Sanjay, I have an idea.'

'And what is that?'

By now, Leena had shifted to a rented apartment in Lokhandwala complex. Since she had no work and her day comprised just meeting Sanjay, she had a lot of time to observe people around her.

'We need three things to lead a good life: a house, a car and money to buy food. Right?'

'Yes.'

'I have a plan. Let's start with getting some cash and jewellery.'

'How?' Sanjay was interested. He had an idea where all this was going, but he wanted to hear what she had to say.

'Remember, you once introduced me to Arup Dey? He works at the airport or something. I found out from Arup that his family keeps a lot of jewellery and cash in their house.'

'I hope you aren't fucking him?'

'Are you jealous? Can you get anything in Mumbai without fucking?'

'I'm jealous, yes, but we need money, so tell me.'

'The fucking is work, honey. It's called a honeytrap.'

Sanjay merely nodded.

'Okay, all we need to do is kill Arup. Once he is dead, we get rid of his body, call his father and tell him to bring us all the money he can to save his son.'

Sanjay remained silent. Even though he had contemplated killing for money, he had never discussed it with anyone. But now, they had no money and nothing on the horizon.

The two of them made a plan.

The next time Arup visited the restaurant, Sanjay convinced him to come to Mahabaleshwar with him. On the way there, Sanjay added sleeping pills to Arup's drink. Once he was drowsy, Sanjay killed Arup and disposed of his body in the Western Ghats. After that, he returned to Mumbai, met Leena the next day, and told her that the operation had gone smoothly.

Next, they had to kill the father.

Two days after killing Arup, Sanjay called his father and said, 'Uncle, the police have arrested your son on the Mumbai–Goa highway. Please come here with money and jewellery. I have a lawyer with me. Please come soon.' He gave the father a location on the outskirts of Mumbai.

Both Arup and his father knew Sanjay well since they frequented his restaurant. The father, therefore, didn't suspect any foul play and rushed to the location Sanjay had given him. Arup was a union leader of the airport employees and his confrontation with the police was a likely possibility, he thought.

Once the father arrived at the location, Sanjay killed him too, took all the money and jewellery he had brought with him and got rid of the body. After that, he returned to Mumbai.

It was a well-executed operation and both Leena and Sanjay were happy.

For the Mumbai Police, this was a high-profile case of a son and father disappearing within two days. Once the bodies were discovered, the police pressed all resources to track down the killer. With the help of eyewitnesses and evidence collected from the scene of crimes, it took them no time to find who was behind the killings.

A few weeks later, a police team arrived and took Sanjay away. By now, Leena had changed her name to Simi Bhatia. She didn't come into the net of the investigation as she had not actively participated in the crime.

The year was 1998 and the charge sheet was filed the following year. The hearings took place over the next three years and Sanjay was convicted for the two murders and sentenced to life imprisonment. Soon after, he was sent to Kolhapur Central Jail.

The five years that Sanjay spent in judicial custody were difficult for Simi. She did everything she could to get a role in a film but was unsuccessful. Desperate and worried that she would have to return to Ludhiana, she began to explore other avenues of making a quick buck. The first thing that came to her mind was cricket.

Betting on cricket matches provided her with an opportunity that she grabbed with both hands. She realized that people's craze for cricket made them willing to spend any amount of money on the game and players would stoop to any level to benefit from this. She met bookies at parties, befriended them, slept with many and became their honeytrap to influence cricketers to perform just as the bookies pleased.

But her heart was in Kolhapur. Under her alias—Simi— she visited Sanjay many times and hired an expensive lawyer. The verdict of the lower court was challenged. It was pointed out that the court had convicted Sanjay on the basis of circumstantial evidence. There was no proof and the prosecution had merely relied on the statements of the witnesses, it was argued. The Mumbai High Court, however, rejected their plea and upheld the sentence.

Eight months later, Sanjay moved an application seeking a two-month parole, stating that his mother was unwell. This was approved.

Sanjay returned to Mumbai and had an emotional reunion with Simi.

'How are you doing, honey?'

She ran into his arms and sobbed as she said, 'Not good. I have missed you.'

Later, she asked him, 'What are you going to do now, Sanjay?'

'I'm not going back to that jail, that's for sure.'

'I don't want you to go either. Can we not do something?'

They discussed several options.

Finally, Simi said, 'The best option is for you to change your name, escape from India and change your appearance when you come back. You will then have a new name and a new face. No one will ever know that you are *you*.'

She laughed and he joined her.

A few days later, Sanjay had a new passport that identified him as Ravi Rana.

He told Simi, 'I'm going to Bangkok to join Santosh Shetty's gang.'

'When will you be back?'

'Soon, I promise.'

Between 2003 and 2006, Sanjay, now with a new identity, made several visits to Mumbai to meet Simi. She became his honeytrap, identifying wealthy single men, befriending them and learning pertinent details about their wealth during their weakest moments in bed. She passed on these minute details to Sanjay so he could start his ruthless threat and recovery actions. Together, they accumulated plenty of money and finally, in some ways, Simi's dreams started to take shape.

In 2003, she was offered a role in a small-budget Bollywood movie. She gave it her best, but the movie was a failure. It was screened at just one cinema hall and turned out to be a disaster. But that didn't deter Simi. She now had money and the thrill of doing what she was doing was far more addictive than acting in films.

But in 2006, her dreams were once again shattered when there was a knock at the door of her house. At that time, Sanjay was with her. Since they had nothing to fear and all was going smoothly, she opened the door. A police team was standing there. They pushed their way in and arrested Sanjay.

Apparently his altered appearance had failed to deceive Arup Dey's sister who had identified him a few days before. The police sent Sanjay back to Kolhapur Central Jail. Once again, Simi was left to fend for herself.

She would often go to meet Sanjay in jail and the two started to make plans to get him out.

Meanwhile, in Mumbai, a new avenue was about to mature. It was called the Indian Premier League, the IPL.

Her bookie contacts got in touch with her again. There would be more money this time, they said, and shorter matches, all played in the evening so that the viewership was larger. Hundreds of players would be involved. Cricket was no longer a game; it was a full-blown entertainment apparatus.

For Simi, this couldn't have been better-timed. She hung out at parties once again, dressed seductively, drank a lot of wine, did drugs with some players if they wanted and became an important link between players and bookies. She also met many Bollywood stars at IPL parties, clicked pictures with them and populated them on social media.

But Simi never forgot Sanjay. She hired a better lawyer this time and was finally successful in getting Sanjay out of jail on the argument that he had been imprisoned for nine years. The court allowed him to go and the police failed to point out the facts to them. Somehow, the lawyers were able to hoodwink everyone that Sanjay was in jail all the time whereas he had actually jumped parole.

The year was 2009, and once again, Sanjay was a free man.

'Darling, you are just amazing.' He hugged her.

'Thank you.' She batted her false eyelashes at him.

'But tell me, what have you been up to? You look so hot. Hotter than before.'

'I'm just the same, honey. You have been in jail for three years and need to have some fun.'

He laughed and they went to her new apartment. She now lived in an upscale apartment in Oshiwara.

He swept her into his arms as soon as they entered and carried her to the bedroom.

After they were spent, Sanjay remarked, 'You look gorgeous.'

'I keep my machinery well-oiled,' she winked as he pulled her closer.

Simi had actually been to Dubai twice to consult a plastic surgeon. The surgeries had corrected minor flaws in her face and body.

This time, Sanjay found it difficult to get back into the Shetty gang and was therefore dependent on Simi. However, he soon learnt of a new opportunity. One of his uncles, Laxman Gite, worked with Mumbai's crime branch. He was an inspector and had solved several important cases.

Sanjay met Gite one day who said, 'Sanjay, you need to stay clean now.'

'That's fine, uncle, but who will give me a job? I have no money and you know my parents are not in a position to help me. What should I do?'

'Why don't you become a *khabari* [informer]?'

Sanjay knew what a khabari was, but he was also aware that criminals hated them.

His uncle continued, 'As a khabari, you can sell information to us. We will pay you and the police will protect you and keep you out of trouble.'

The idea appealed to him. He could earn money while he continued to do what he wanted to without getting caught by the police. He loved the immunity part the most.

'Uncle, I agree with you. Just keep me away from trouble.'

'I promise.'

Sanjay soon realized that being a khabari was tough. The pay was low, the risk was high, and on top of that, a gang could bump him off at any time.

Even though he continued to see Simi, the two of them started to drift apart. There was no specific reason, but he was happy that she was doing well even as he was dragging his feet. In any case, Simi had helped him so many times that this time he had decided to do something on his own.

One day, Sanjay met a German woman and the two fell in love instantly. Sanjay, who was feeling rootless at the time, away from his world of crime, discovered a new anchor. The woman was beautiful, spoke with a weird accent that he found amusing and was great in bed. After a month of courtship, the two got married. It was love at first sight and everything happened quickly.

Obviously, after he got married, he kept his distance from Simi even more.

But after a few months, unable to make any money at all, Sanjay again turned to Simi and they decided to continue with the honeytrap method of making money.

One day, Simi said, 'Remember that joker Varun Kukreja? He owes me forty lakhs.'

'I remember him; he writes for films and composes songs. So he owes you forty lakhs? Let's take it then.'

'But the problem is that he has no money.'

'What does he owe you for?'

'Lost cricket bets.'

'We shouldn't let him go. He has cheated you. What does he have? A house? Jewellery?'

'Nothing, he is a *fukra* [broke]. He is staying in a rented flat, his parents live in Delhi and . . . wait a minute, he does have a BMW.'

'And how much is that model worth?'

'Approximately forty lakhs.'

'So, let's just take it from him.'

They decided to kill Varun Kukreja. It was 2012.

Varun was an aspiring movie producer and Simi told him that Sanjay could set up a meeting with a potential financier, someone who would finance his production house.

But there was no financier. Sanjay and two other men he introduced as his friends went to Varun's house on the pretext of taking him for the meeting. They rode in Varun's BMW, heading towards Pune. On a lonely stretch, Sanjay asked Varun to stop the car. They took him to a spot far away from the road and gave him two options.

'Varun, you have to die. But as a friend, I am giving you two options. Select one. Should I slit your throat while you are conscious or would you like to swallow these sleeping pills, fall unconscious and then we kill you?'

Varun cried and begged for mercy. Finally, he gave up. 'Give me the pills.'

As soon as he was unconscious, Sanjay slit his throat. Then they cut his body into five parts and threw it in the ghats.

After this, Sanjay tried to sell the BMW using his contacts. He drove the car into Pune and waited for his contact. But when no one turned up, the three of them abandoned the car in a deserted area and took a bus back to Mumbai.

Simi was furious. 'Sanjay, why did you abandon the car?'

Sanjay showed her the credit cards he had stolen from Varun. 'We have these at least.'

'But these won't help us recover the money.'

'I know, but I couldn't have brought the car back to Mumbai. It was too risky.'

Sanjay began to wonder if Simi was jealous of his wife and was therefore overreacting.

But Sanjay and Simi had a long association and he immediately dismissed the thought.

In fact, for Varun Kukreja, Sanjay was Varun Bhatia, Simi's brother. Ever since Sanjay got married, that was how Simi introduced him to their targets.

Once Kukreja was out of the way, Sanjay used his credit cards to buy clothes from Inorbit mall in Andheri and also used it at a few places during a visit to Bangkok.

Little did Sanjay know that, in Delhi, Kukreja's brother would learn of these transactions. The brother had lodged a missing person's complaint with the Mumbai Police, but no progress had been made.

He decided to go to Mumbai. The first place he visited was Inorbit mall. He knew the time of the purchases from the statements he had received and reviewed CCTV footage—provided by the mall security—corresponding to those times. It was painstaking work, but he was finally able to narrow down on a list of suspects, details of which he shared with the police.

Meanwhile, Simi and Sanjay were planning their next crime. Their target this time was a small-time actor, Agraj Tikam. He had got close to Simi, whom Sanjay had introduced as his sister.

Agraj owned three flats in an upscale residential locality worth several crores, the reason why Sanjay was interested in him.

Sanjay had convinced him that Simi would get him good roles in movies using her contacts if he rented out two flats to his friends for free. Agraj agreed and Sanjay got two of his assistants to move in.

Agraj's father, who lived in Delhi, came to know of this and confronted his son as he wanted to approve who his son rented the flats to. He ordered him to cancel the agreement and get rid of the tenants. When Agraj conveyed this to Sanjay, Sanjay had another agreement made in the name of his German wife, hoping that an international name would make the old man less suspicious of the tenants. But Agraj's father was not happy about this either and landed in Mumbai one day. He then evicted Sanjay's assistants from the flats.

This left both Simi and Sanjay furious.

'Saala buddha [old man], what does he think of himself?'

Simi nodded.

Sanjay continued, 'I will convince Agraj to leave Mumbai tonight. Let the men do their job.'

Sanjay's wife had already moved back to Germany as the marriage was not working out.

He called Agraj. 'Yaar, Agraj. I have a good film offer for you.'

'Really? Thanks, bhai.'

'But you will have to leave for Goa with me this evening. The producer is there and wants to meet you in person. Are you ready to leave today?'

'Yes, bhai. Thanks!'

Sanjay met Simi in the afternoon. 'Simi, father and son hate each other. Let's make sure Agraj is arrested for his father's murder. Once that happens and, as soon as he gets bail, we should make him commit suicide.'

'That's smart. But tell me, how can we achieve this?'

Sanjay explained his plan to Simi. But it was not complete. Sanjay confessed, 'The first part, getting Agraj arrested for the murder of his father, is easy, but the second part is tricky. How will we make him commit suicide? Do you have any ideas, Simi?'

'I will handle it. Leave it to me, my brother.'

Simi had once got Agraj to write a suicide note when he was high on cocaine. They had been role-playing at the time. She was sure he wouldn't remember writing it. The note was in her locker at the bank.

Sanjay was relieved and the plan was set in motion.

That evening, as soon as Agraj left the society in his car to pick Sanjay up, Sanjay's assistants—the same two people who had been kicked out by Agraj's father—entered Agraj's flat. They had a bag containing knives.

Agraj's father raised an alarm as soon as he realized their intentions, but the killers struck. Before help could come, they had escaped through the bathroom window and vanished into the night.

The next morning, the murder became big news, thanks to the upscale locality where the crime had been committed.

The primary suspect was Agraj Tikam. His neighbours told the police that he often argued and fought with his father and was the last person they had seen with the old man.

The police tried to reach him on his mobile, but it was switched off. Roadblocks were set up, entry and exits points were watched and all-out efforts to arrest the killer were launched.

Sanjay and Simi's plan had gone well except that the murder had not been smooth. The guard told the police that he had heard a man crying for help.

'Sahib, I heard someone shouting for help. The voice came from Tikam Sahib's house. I informed the supervisor and both of us went there and knocked on the door. It was opened by the tenants who had been asked to vacate a few days ago. They were Agraj Sir's friends. They said there was no trouble and told us to go away.'

Thanks to the guard's statement, the police realized that Agraj was not the killer. By then Agraj had been arrested and the media had already declared him the murderer based on Mumbai Police's initial reports. The police launched a manhunt for the two tenants. They were picked up in Satara the next day. They pointed a finger at their boss, Sanjay Ranade.

Sanjay was arrested again. This was a setback. He maintained his cool and insisted that he was innocent. He was lucky that his uncle was a part of the team that had arrested him. When he was brought into the crime branch compound in Andheri, his uncle had winked at him. Sanjay knew what he had to do. He had not been handcuffed as the police were only taking him in for questioning.

As soon as he stepped out of the jeep, he ran. The policemen chased him, but he escaped.

He boarded a local train for Churchgate and called a senior police officer he had passed on a lot of information to as a khabari. It was time to encash the favour.

'Sir, I need help. I want to get out of India. Just help me one last time.'

The senior officer declined and hung up. Sanjay called Simi next. 'Simi, yaar, we are in trouble. Help me, please.'

'Yes, Sanjay, what do you want me to do?'

'I need to hide in a hotel room. I can't use my own name. Someone will have to pay for me and check me in under their name. Can you do that?'

Simi's razor-sharp mind came up with a solution. She knew a man, Geetam Arora. He was a stockbroker and his girlfriend had committed suicide because he had fallen for Simi.

'Yes, give me a few minutes.'

Simi had introduced Sanjay to Geetam as her brother. Geetam had taken Simi to meet his family and was keen to meet Simi's. Since she could not take him to Ludhiana, she had introduced Sanjay as her brother, Varun Bhatia.

Simi called Geetam. 'Honey, I need help. My brother, Varun, is in trouble. The police are harassing him. Can you please do something? He just needs to lie low for a few hours.'

'Yes, honey. Give me a minute . . . Okay, tell him to go to Hotel Goldwin in Colaba. By the time he reaches there, I will have fixed everything.'

Simi called Sanjay and told him where to go.

She was sure Sanjay would be able to hoodwink the police once again and get out of India.

After a few hours, she turned on the TV and was shocked to see the news. Both Sanjay and Geetam had been taken into custody. This meant the police could come knocking at her door at any moment. She got up and looked through the peephole, but there was no one around.

She looked at herself in the mirror. Even though she knew she had to get out as fast as she could, she couldn't leave the house without looking her best. She changed her dress, did her hair and spent some time applying make-up. Once done, she looked at herself and smiled. She looked gorgeous.

Simi picked up her bag and walked towards the door. As soon as she opened it, she saw a team of four waiting there. Two men and two women in khaki. One of the women, an inspector, announced, 'You are under arrest, Miss Simi.'

Interesting fact: Simi was granted bail. No one knows her current whereabouts. Sanjay finally confessed to killing Varun Kukreja and informed the police about where he had disposed of the body. The police recovered a head, torso and a few bones. While some bones were identified as those of an animal in the forensic report, the head and the torso appeared to be of two different people. While one of them could have been Kukreja's, the police could not identify the other person. Based on these findings, the police charged Sanjay with three murders: Agraj Tikam's father, Varun Kukreja and one more person they were unable to identify. But due to the complexity of the case and the misleading information that Sanjay had been feeding to the police, to date, not one case has progressed.

10

The Baby Killers

Sanjana Bai Govil was nervous as she waited for her husband in their small, one-room house in Pune. Her two daughters, Ambika and Meena, were sitting next to her. It was 8 p.m.

Around 8.30 p.m., Sohan, her husband, walked in. He looked at Sanjana as she avoided meeting his eyes.

'You bitch,' his voice was hoarse, as if he was exercising restraint because of the presence of his young daughters. 'Because of you, I have to lose face.'

Sanjana remained quiet. She knew what would follow.

'I'm an ex-army man and, for me, honour means everything. Why can't you stop this?' He was standing right next to her, his breath warm on her face. Sanjana kept her eyes glued to the floor.

Meena, who was just ten, began to cry. Sohan continued to stare at his wife.

'Answer me!' This time, his voice was loud enough to be heard outside.

Sanjana looked up, met his eye and dropped her gaze once again.

Sohan slapped her. 'You whore! Why can't you stop stealing? How much beating do you need?'

With this, he pushed both their daughters out of the house, closed the front door and turned to look at his wife once again. His eyes were red and he was shaking with anger.

Outside, the daughters hugged each other and began to cry. As the dreadful sounds of pain increased from within the house, so did their sobbing. They lived in a chawl with too many people packed into a small area. A few concerned neighbours stopped near the door and looked pitifully at the girls. One old woman sat down next to them and pulled them close. The girls, helpless and confused, wailed even louder as they placed their heads on the woman's shoulder.

Sohan emerged ten minutes later. By now, almost fifty people had gathered outside the house. All eyes were on him. No one said anything. No one ever said anything because they felt he was right. A woman who was a thief had to be dealt with.

Within minutes, all of them went their own way. The show had ended. Hopefully, there would be no more unpleasant sights like this, but all they could do was hope. All Sohan could also do was hope.

He nodded at the old woman, who was the last person remaining, and holding his daughters' hands went back inside the house and closed the door.

Sanjana was on the floor. Hearing them enter, she tried to get up but couldn't. Sohan looked at his daughters and smiled.

'Let's have dinner. Are you hungry?'

Both nodded. They were not hungry, but both knew that saying 'no' was not an option. Sanjana had prepared roti and bhaji. Sohan served his daughters and himself, and they began to eat. Sanjana stayed where she was.

The next morning, Sohan went to the police station and met Inspector Deshmukh.

'Inspector Sahib, she won't steal from today. I promise. Just let her go one last time.'

The inspector looked at him and said without a smile, 'Sohan, I admire your patience. Your wife has been pickpocketing at railway stations and temples for so many years now and you still think she can change?'

Sohan remained silent. In his heart, he knew that he was part of the problem. He had no job. In fact, wherever he worked, he was soon fired. All he had was his pension, which was not enough to support the family.

'I am confident this time, Inspector Sahib.'

From the police station, he walked to a nearby municipality park. He was smiling now. He pulled out a comb from his back pocket and, as he walked, combed his hair. Next, he opened the top button of his shirt and flicked the collar up.

The reason for this change in demeanour was the prospect of meeting his girlfriend, Pratibha. He had met Pratibha a few months ago at a fair. The two were in love. Not happy with Sanjana, who was not changing her ways, Pratibha was his relief valve.

She smiled as soon as she saw him and his own smile widened, the memory of the previous night forgotten.

Sohan had bought a garland of fresh jasmine flowers, which he put in Pratibha's hair as she sat beside him, demure and giggling.

They sat in the park for a couple of hours, eating bhelpuri and sipping tender coconut water. Late in the afternoon, the two of them went to watch a movie. After seeing her off, as Sohan was walking back to his house, he realized that his temper was beginning to rise again and his headache was back.

While Meena, the younger of the two daughters, was born to Sohan and Sanjana, the elder one, Ambika, was from Sanjana's previous marriage. Originally from Nashik, Sanjana had eloped with a truck driver and come to Pune fifteen years ago, where Ambika was born. The man she had eloped with abandoned her soon after. She later married Sohan. When he had found out about her habit of stealing, she had said it was poverty that had pushed her towards petty crime.

That evening when Sohan returned home, all was normal. Sanjana was waiting for him, flowers in her hair. The aroma of freshly prepared dinner greeted him. His daughters smiled fondly at him. He relaxed a bit.

A few weeks passed without any incident. Every day, when he returned home after meeting Pratibha, he was given the same welcome.

But slowly, he began to realize that his anger at Sanjana was not just because of her stealing, but also the result of his attraction for Pratibha. He wanted to leave Sanjana and marry Pratibha, but it was not going to be easy. He had no idea what to do.

One evening, while the family was eating dinner, Sanjana said, 'Sohan, we need to pay the school fees for Ambika and Meena.'

He looked up but said nothing. He had no money.

'If we don't pay by tomorrow, they will not be allowed to attend the school.'

He stopped eating and looked at Sanjana. 'You know I don't have work, don't you? From where should I get this money then?'

Sanjana was angry. It was not her concern where he got the money from; as the head of the family, he had to find ways to earn. 'So, why don't you work?'

He pushed his plate aside violently. Some of the dal and bhaji spilled on to the floor.

'You know I have been looking for work. If I can't find any, what can I do?'

Sanjana glared at him. 'That bitch Pratibha won't give you work. You have to look for work in offices.'

At the mention of his girlfriend's name, Sohan's temper flared. 'How dare you?'

Sanjana kept her eyes on him. 'You are fucking another woman while I wait for you at home. And now you are telling me you don't have the money for our children's education?'

He hit her. But this time, Sanjana was in a different mood. Ever since she had learnt of her husband's affair, something had changed within her. She picked up a rolling pin and hit him on the head.

Sohan cried out in pain and looked at her, unsure of what to do next. She hit him again and again. He placed his hands over his head to protect it, the blood flowing through his fingers and down his forehead. After a few hits, he managed to crawl out through the door to the safety of the outside world.

Sanjana closed the door and returned to sit near her girls. She picked up her plate of unfinished dinner, looked at her daughters, smiled and nodded. The three resumed eating.

Sohan didn't return. In fact, Sanjana later learnt that he had married Pratibha and moved to Nashik. She felt cheated and demeaned and decided to take revenge.

Since she didn't have a job and her daughters were too young to work, she decided to fall back on stealing. But this time, she trained her daughters as well. They became a gang of three, specializing in purse-snatching, chain-snatching, pickpocketing and shoplifting. The mother taught the girls all the tricks of the trade.

Everything was going smoothly till something unusual happened one day. The year was 1990. Sanjana was at home and her daughters were on the prowl near a famous temple in Pune. The sisters, now in their twenties, had become experts. They always worked together. Ambika was married to a man named Kavi Barve and they had a three-year-old son, Ashish. Their modus operandi was simple: Kavi would wait near the exit of the temple in his Fiat while the sisters identified their target, executed the theft and escaped to the waiting car. That afternoon, Ambika had Ashish with her. She identified her target, but as soon as she snatched her chain, the woman raised a hue and cry. The devotees surrounded Ambika and her son.

Ambika stealthily dropped the chain on the floor and started to shout, 'I have not stolen anything! This woman is lying.'

But the crowd was not convinced. The victim was an old woman and looked pious. Surely she would not lie. Ambika felt trapped and pleaded, 'I'm a mother.' She pointed to her son. 'You think a mother who has come to a temple to seek the blessings of god would steal?'

That did the trick. The people in the crowd looked at one another and nodded. Someone then spotted the gold chain on the marble floor. The old woman said it was hers. The crowd began to disperse and Ambika, along with her son, moved towards the exit. Meena, who had been watching the developments from among the crowd, breathed easy and followed her sister.

'Narrow escape. Drive,' Ambika said to Kavi as soon as she and Meena sat in the car.

Little did they know that this incident would become the foundation on which a very dangerous and evil plan would be made, a strategy so dangerous that it would rattle criminals across the world, and indeed have no parallel in India's recorded crime history.

After they reached home, they told Sanjana what had happened at the temple. After mulling over their account for a few minutes, Sanjana finally said, 'I think we have been given a sign. You were at a temple and god has shown us a way to carry out our operations more efficiently.'

'What do you mean, ma?' asked Meena.

'From now onwards, we will use young children as shields.'

Ambika raised her eyebrows. 'Shields? But Ashish will be at school and there are no other children in the family.'

'We will kidnap them.'

The three looked at each other as Sanjana continued, 'There are far too many unwanted children in this world.' She paused and her expression hardened.

'Ma?' prompted Meena.

Sanjana looked at Meena. Her eyes were distant and cold, her expression hard to decipher.

She took a deep breath and said, her voice level, 'We must start with Nashik.'

'Nashik?' The three of them said together.

'Bring that traitor's daughter to me first.'

'You mean . . .' Meena hesitated before continuing, 'My father's daughter?'

Sanjana looked at her and nodded.

No one spoke for a few minutes. Finally, Sanjana continued, steel in her voice, 'He is no longer your father, Meena. Understood? I am your father, and I am your mother. For our family, he is dead. But now is the time for us to teach him a lesson for abandoning us. Bastard, he left all of us for another woman.'

The plan was finalized and the three of them took a bus to Nashik the next day. They reached Sohan's house where he now lived with his new wife and their three-year-old daughter, Sapna. They hid at a little distance from the house and began their wait for the right opportunity. It was 4 p.m. and there was hardly anyone in the vicinity as it was an exceptionally hot day. Finally, around 5 p.m., a few kids came out to play.

Ambika approached them and even though she had seen one of them come out of Sohan's house, she had to be certain. 'Is your name Sapna?'

The girl nodded and Ambika looked around. There was no adult in sight. She pulled a chocolate out of her bag. 'You want this?'

The little girl accepted the chocolate.

'You want more?'

The girl nodded again and followed Ambika to the corner where Meena and Kavi were waiting. Meena quickly hailed an autorickshaw and the three of them sat in it, taking the girl with them. They headed straight to the bus stand. The girl didn't create any trouble. She innocently looked out at the passing traffic, eating her chocolate, a trace of a smile on her face.

By the time they boarded the bus, Sapna had started to get restless. Not sure what they would do if she raised an alarm, Ambika fed her well. They were relieved when the girl dozed off. They were in their home in Pune before she woke up.

When Sapna finally woke up, Sanjana focused her attention on her. Kavi had gone out to buy vegetables, taking his son, and only the mother and her two daughters were in the house with Sapna.

The little girl rubbed her eyes and looked around. Seeing unfamiliar surroundings, she began to cry. Meena picked her up and tried to calm her down. But Sanjana snatched Sapna from her daughter's arms.

'This is the poisonous seed that that bastard has grown.'

With this, she started to bang the little girl's head against the wall. The girl started to cry hysterically in pain and shock, but Sanjana didn't stop. Ambika and Meena looked at their mother in horror, but they didn't dare to say anything. After a few minutes, when the girl fell silent, Sanjana dropped her to the floor. By now, the wall was smeared with blood and so were Sanjana's sari, face and arms. A few drops had splashed on to the sisters too.

Sanjana took a bath and washed her sari, while the sisters cleaned the wall and the floor. Then they put Sapna's body in a gunny bag and waited.

When Sanjana came out of the bathroom, she instructed them, 'Clean up and get rid of this.'

The sisters bathed and as they were about to leave with the body, Kavi returned with Ashish.

He realized what had happened. 'Are you out of your mind?'

He looked at Sanjana who just stared at him. Kavi fell quiet and the sisters left the house with the gunny bag.

In Nashik, Sohan's wife filed a missing person's report with the police. In her report, she stated that she suspected Sanjana, but the case made no progress as the search by the local police yielded no results.

In Pune, a week later, confident now about kidnapping a child, Sanjana ordered her daughters to kidnap another one. Within a few days, as soon as the gang spotted an unattended child in a temple, Ambika pounced on him. There were far too many people in the temple at that time to notice. Within a few minutes the gang was driving towards their home after another successful kidnapping.

This child, who was a boy of around eight months, became their shield for the next few weeks. The sisters went about their business of stealing with one of them holding the baby. After a few successful thefts, Ambika was caught by a couple. She whistled to Meena who was holding the boy.

On hearing the whistle, Meena dropped the baby on to the floor. The child began to cry loudly, creating much-needed distraction. As the attention of the crowd was diverted, Ambika fled the scene. Meena picked up the child, made a show of soothing him, accepted water from one of the devotees, thanked everyone and walked towards the getaway car.

While the gang was successful in saving themselves by the skin of their teeth, they were not aware of a new problem that awaited them. The force with which the child fell had caused internal bleeding in his brain. He kept crying despite all efforts to calm him down. They got out of the car, the child crying uncontrollably, and went inside their house.

'What happened?' Sanjana demanded.

'We had to drop him to cause a distraction and now he won't stop crying,' Ambika said.

Ambika and Kavi's son was playing outside at that time.

The women tried to make the child comfortable and gave him some milk. But it was of no use. After half an hour, fed up and worried that the neighbours might come asking what the matter was, Sanjana looked at her daughters and said, 'Kill him.'

This time, the sisters didn't hesitate. They walked towards the child, picked up a towel and smothered him. He was dead in less than a minute.

The room became quiet and they realized that they were hungry. Meena had bought vada pav for all of them. They ate gratefully as they watched a movie on the small TV in their house, the body of the child between their legs on the floor.

It was a day well spent. Only one thing remained to be done—to dispose of the body. After the movie ended, it was time for work. The sisters picked up the body, wrapped it in a towel and threw it in a dustbin a little distance from where they lived. Kavi once again drove the car.

Kavi did not like this ugly turn of events. He was okay with minor thefts, but the kidnaping and killing of children troubled his conscience. However, he was in love with Ambika. They had a lovely son and she was carrying their second child. One day, he took her out for dinner to a famous pav-bhaji restaurant with the intention of raising his concern.

After they had eaten, he said, 'Ambika, I love you. You know that, don't you?'

She smiled and nodded.

'So, I'm going to tell you something that has been troubling me. Since I love you, I don't want to keep it within me. Okay?'

She continued to smile and nodded.

'I think we are committing a great sin by killing these children. We have already killed two. God will punish us, Ambika. We must stop this.'

Ambika was no longer smiling. 'Kavi, what are you saying? We have killed no one. We merely obeyed Ma's orders.'

'But it is still a sin, sweetheart.'

'No, it isn't. Ma is the ultimate. If I don't follow her instructions, who will? Will God pardon us if we disobey our own mother's orders, disobey the orders of the one who created us?'

This was not going well for him. 'Mom is supreme, I agree, but she can't ask us to kill people.'

Ambika scanned his face before she said, 'I'm surprised you are even saying this.'

'Ambika, I agree she is important. But what about me?'

'Your orders are important, but my mother's orders are more important. You can't even imagine what she has been through.'

That evening, as the couple fell quiet, staring out through the window of the restaurant, their faces turned away from one another, Kavi learnt a rude lesson—Sanjana's ways had to be accepted if he wished to continue living with Ambika.

He looked at Ambika. Even now, after all that they had said to each other, he wasn't angry with her. He was angry at the situation, but not with her. Kavi loved her so much that he decided to drop the topic and play along. They ate ice cream and, by the time they walked back to the car, they were holding hands.

Over the next six years, they abducted several children and used them as shields. Sanjana expanded their operations to other cities, including Kolhapur, Mumbai and Thane. As soon as a child was no longer useful or fell sick or created too much trouble, they killed the child and kidnapped another.

Although Sanjana had more than 150 cases registered against her, they were all for petty theft and the police had nothing on her daughters. This kept them off the radar.

From 1990 to 1996, dozens of children went missing in various cities across Maharashtra, but the police could not connect the dots and attribute the abductions to a single gang. Also, most of the children abducted and killed belonged to poor families. Being uneducated, almost all the parents were unable to lodge formal complaints.

Then, in 1996, emboldened by their success, Sanjana proposed a daring mission. She had learnt that her ex-husband, Sohan, had become a father again. Ever since she had heard about this, she hadn't been able to sleep. Since she couldn't do anything to Sohan, whom she hated from the bottom of her heart, she decided to kill his second child too.

Sanjana looked at her daughters and her son-in-law and declared, 'We have to kidnap that bastard's child.'

The three nodded as she continued, 'We have to do it as soon as possible. Leave tomorrow. Go by taxi this time and be careful.'

They nodded again.

Meanwhile, sensing that Sanjana might strike, Sohan's wife was taking every precaution. Even though she had told the police that she suspected Sanjana for Sapna's kidnapping, the police had done nothing about it. All they had said was that since the suspect lived in another town, they had sent the file to that district for action. No action was ever taken. But this time, she could trust no one.

She said to Sohan one day, 'I think that bitch Sanjana will try and do something to our child.'

'How do you know?'

'Call it intuition.'

'We have to be very careful then. I don't trust her either. She is mad and capable of doing anything.' Sohan rubbed his head, remembering the wound he had received after Sanjana beat him up.

The gang arrived in Nashik early one morning. They drove past the colony where Sohan and his family lived. Everything was quiet. By now, all three could easily identify policemen in plain clothes.

This time the operation was more difficult compared to the last time as the child was just an infant and would not step out to play. They had no option but to wait for the right opportunity. After parking the taxi at a little distance from Sohan's house, they sat chatting, watching the front door of the house. Around 10 a.m., they saw Sohan emerge with a bag. It appeared that he was on his way to office. As he walked towards them, the three of them ducked. Once he was gone, they waited for ten minutes before asking the driver to proceed closer to the gate.

Instructing him to keep the engine running, the three got out and knocked at the door. Since no one opened it, they knocked again.

The trio had no idea that Sohan had spotted them in the taxi.

Sohan's wife finally opened the door. She was holding an infant in her arms. This opportunity was a godsend. Ambika attacked her even before the woman could react and pulled the infant away from her. Then she turned and walked back quickly towards the taxi. That was when she saw Sohan running towards them, accompanied by a few policemen.

The three were arrested and taken to the police station. The police questioned them but could get no information. Finally, late that night, Meena gave in. Based on her statements, they cornered the other two but didn't make much progress.

The next day, the Nashik police got a court order to search the premises of the Govil sisters in Pune. The investigating team came across many items of children's clothing and several photographs. The children in these photographs resembled the children who had gone missing over the years.

As soon as the news was leaked to the media, it became a high-profile case. Investigation was handed over to the CID (Crime Investigation Department).

Over the next few weeks, a team of CID officers painstakingly pieced together the gory details of the serial killings the Govil family had carried out. But to prepare a watertight case, they needed inside help.

While Meena had been the first to talk in Nashik, she turned mute after she met Sanjana, who was arrested and brought to the jail too. The CID team's last hope was Kavi. They pressed their best officer, Inspector Sachit Damle, into service.

Sachit had more than a decade of experience in the police, of which he had spent almost five years in the CID. He was tall, almost six feet, with broad shoulders and hooded eyebrows under which his eyes were always red. Just meeting his eyes was enough to send a shiver down a person's spine.

Sachit met Kavi in the interrogation room and said in his deep voice, 'I'm your last and only hope if you want to escape the death sentence.'

The silence grew around Kavi. He was sure he would be hanged and cursed himself for being foolish enough to have abetted the crimes. He had also fathered four children with Ambika and the weight of this responsibility was playing on his mind.

'Do you want to live?'

He nodded, looked up, but couldn't stand the intensity of Sachit's eyes. He dropped his gaze again.

'Become an approver and you can walk free.'

'Approver?'

'Yes, tell us everything, from the beginning, in detail, and we will grant you immunity.'

Kavi agreed immediately. His anger at Sanjana made it easy for him to do so. He knew he could not save his wife, but if he was not in jail, he could at least take care of their children.

'I'm very sorry, sir. I will tell you everything. Please . . .' he started to cry bitterly.

Sachit's job was done. The police filed the charge sheet and the hearing was soon held in the sessions court in Pune. On 28 June 2001, the trial court sentenced both Ambika and Meena to death. Sanjana had died in jail in December 1998. No punishment was awarded to Kavi Barve in accordance with what the CID had promised to him.

In September 2004, the Mumbai High Court upheld the sentence. In August 2006, the sentence was further upheld by the Supreme Court of India. The sisters' last ditch effort to seek mercy from the President was also rejected in August 2014. They are currently in Yerawada Central Jail in Pune, awaiting their hanging.

> **Interesting fact:** Not once did Sanjana crack while she was in police custody. During interrogations, she kept her mouth shut and stared at nothing and no one in particular. She had become so thick-skinned that all methods employed by the police to make her speak failed.

Acknowledgements

We wish to thank the police officers across cities and states who opened up about their experiences with us. Though we can't name them, we would like to record our gratitude for the information they shared.

Thanks are also due to the following:

1. Harish Negi, chief librarian at Delhi Gymkhana Club, and his efficient and helpful staff, whom we turned to for rare and out-of-print books.
2. Surender Mohan Pathak ji, the king of Hindi crime fiction, whose knowledge of police procedures and investigation techniques is unparalleled.
3. Suman Arora, lawyer at the Delhi High Court, for the legal insights.
4. Inspector Ajay Kumar Yadav of Delhi Police, who explained to us the practical aspects related to police procedures.
5. Suhail Mathur and the team at The Book Bakers who were with us at every step, from the idea to the execution of the book.

6.   Milee Ashwarya and Aslesha Kadian at Penguin
      Random House India for their wholehearted support
      and guidance.
7.   And, finally, to all those who contributed, directly or
      indirectly, to this book. You know who you are and
      we thank you from the bottom of our hearts.

A Note on the Authors

Sushant Singh

A film and television actor, Sushant Singh hosted the crime-based reality show *Savdhaan India* for almost seven years. He is the honorary general secretary of the Cine & TV Artistes' Association. This is his first book.

Kulpreet Yadav

A bestselling author and motivational speaker, Kulpreet Yadav retired voluntarily from the armed forces to pursue a career in writing in 2014. He was the winner of the Best Fiction Writer for 2018 award at the Gurgaon Literature Festival. He lives in New Delhi.